Nanking Letters, 1949

NANKING
LETTERS
1949

Knight Biggerstaff

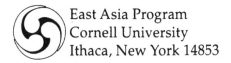
East Asia Program
Cornell University
Ithaca, New York 14853

The Cornell East Asia Series is published by the Cornell University East Asia Program and has no formal affiliation with Cornell University Press. We are a small, non-profit press, publishing reasonably-priced books on a variety of scholarly topics relating to East Asia as a service to the academic community and the general public. We accept standing orders which provide for automatic billing and shipping of each title in the series upon publication.

If after review by internal and external readers a manuscript is accepted for publication, it is published on the basis of camera-ready copy provided by the volume author. Each author is thus responsible for any necessary copy-editing and for manuscript formatting.

Submission inquiries should be addressed to Editorial Board, East Asia Program, Cornell University, Ithaca, New York 14853-7601.

Frontispiece: Professor Knight Biggerstaff,
February 1942, courtesy of Cornell University Library
Division of Rare & Manuscript Collections.
COVER DESIGN BY KAREN K. SMITH

Number 23 in the Cornell East Asia Series
© 1979 by Knight Biggerstaff. All rights reserved
Reformatted Edition 2000
ISSN 1050-2955
ISBN 0-939657-23-6 pb

⊗The paper in this book meets the requirements for permanence of ISO 9706:1994

Contents

Introduction 1

The Letters 11

Notes 85

Article "The Nanking Press: April-September 1949" 87

Acknowledgments

I wish to thank my colleagues Charles A. Peterson and Sherman G. Cochran for many helpful suggestions as this material was being prepared for publication. I am also grateful to Richard Gaulton, who has written a Ph.D. dissertation on political mobilization in Shanghai during the early years of the People's Republic, for a list of books on the liberation of that city with most of which I was unfamiliar.

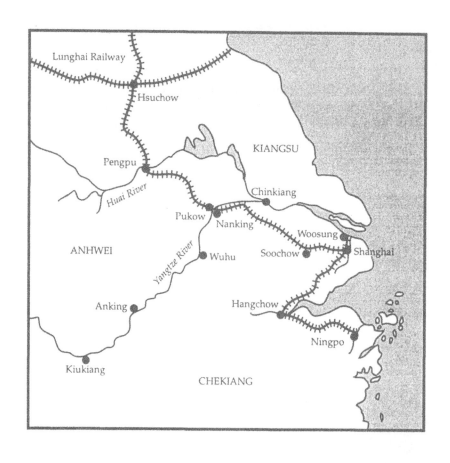

Introduction

The year 1949 is a major milestone in Chinese history because it witnessed the collapse of the Kuomintang National Government on the mainland and the succession to power there of the Chinese Communist Party's People's Government. The bitter civil war that followed the Japanese surrender in 1945 reached a climax in the closing months of 1948 as the more numerous and better equipped but generally badly led armed forces of Generalissimo Chiang Kai-shek were eliminated from Manchuria and from most of North China by the better led and highly indoctrinated People's Liberation Army (PLA) of the Communists. In January 1949 the psychologically significant surrender of Peking and Tientsin occurred, and the last effective Nationalist armies (some 600,000 soldiers, of whom more than half surrendered with their USA-supplied arms and equipment) were crushed in the strategically crucial area between the Lunghai Railway and Huai River. The PLA moved thereafter virtually without opposition to the north bank of the Yangtze River, where it stood poised for further action while its soldiers rested and were resupplied.

Recognizing the weakness of his government's position, Generalissimo Chiang withdrew from Nanking, the Nationalist capital, late in January. While he turned over his presidential responsibilities to Vice President Li Tsung-jen, he continued to exercise control over most of the remaining Nationalist armed forces and the government's monetary reserves. The cabinet, under Premier Sun Fo, also departed, moving to Canton. Vice President Li sent two successive missions north to negotiate a settlement with the Communists, but with the weakness of the National Government so clearly exposed, Chairman Mao Tse-tung insisted upon terms that amounted to a complete surrender and Li declined to accept them. On April 21 the PLA crossed the Yangtze River both above and below Nanking, and the next few days saw the flight of most remaining Nationalist officials and sympathizers, retreating soldiers leaving the city all day on the 23rd.

The Wuhan cities fell on May 16-17 and Shanghai on May 25. Thereafter the PLA moved rapidly south- and westward, occupying Canton on October 14, Chungking on November 30, Nanking on December 4, and Chengtu on December 27. Generalissimo Chiang meanwhile had reassumed the presidency of the National Government and established its offices in Taipei, on the large island of Taiwan, to which 800,000 of the remaining Nationalist army, naval and air forces were transported and to which large numbers of Kuomintang officials and roughly one and one-half million other mainland Chinese made their way. On October 1, 1949 Communist Party Chairman Mao Tse-tung proclaimed the establishment of the People's Republic of China, with Peking as its capital. Except for a few enclaves where resistance continued for awhile and a number of individuals who went into hiding, all Nationalist armies and officials had been captured or swept from the mainland by the end of the year, beginning a new era in Chinese history.[1]

I was able to observe what the Chinese Communists called the liberation of Nanking thanks to a sabbatical leave from Cornell University during the spring semester of 1949, a Rockefeller postwar fellowship, and a Fulbright subsistence grant. I had planned to spend my leave in Peking, carrying on research on the earliest modern Chinese government schools. But the PLA occupied that city before Mrs. Biggerstaff (hereafter Mrs. B) and I could get there. Since our American passport forbade our going to any Communist-held area, we went to Nanking instead arriving there on March 19, after a three day stop in Shanghai. We rented half of a duplex house from the University of Nanking (Chin-ling ta-hsüeh), and I devoted most of my time during the next six months to research in the very fine library of that university's Institute of Chinese Cultural Studies, also visiting the Kiangsu Provincial Library and the library of the Institute of Social Sciences of the Academia Sinica from time to time. The National Central Library and the library of the Institute of History and Philology had already been moved from Nanking to Taiwan.

I was given the fullest cooperation by President Ch'en Yu-kuang and the faculty and staff members of the University of Nanking; Professor Li Siao-yuen, the University Librarian and Director of the Institute, and his staff were especially helpful. Wang Shou-i, a graduate student in history at the National Central University, proved to be a conscientious research assistant, and several University of Nanking students copied materials for me. We found a number of old friends and acquaintances serving in U.S. Government and in Chinese National Government agencies, and met many other interesting people, both Chinese and foreigners.

Among the American friends we saw most often in Nanking and whose names appear frequently in my letters were the Ralph N. Cloughs (Second Secretary of the U.S. embassy, who had been a student of mine at the University of Washington in 1937-38 and a fellow officer in the U.S. embassy in Chungking in 1945-46), Frederick W. (Fritz) Mote (a Fulbright fellow and graduate student at the University of Nanking), the George L. (Bud) Harrises (U.S. Cultural Attaché and Secretary of the U.S. Educational Foundation in China (USEFC)—the Fulbright agency, who had also been a student of mine at the University of Washington in 1937-38), Shirley Duncan (Program Assistant, USEFC, and an old friend), Major Robert Van Ausdall (Assistant U.S. Air Attaché, who had graduated from Cornell the year before with a major in Chinese Studies), and Dr. J. Leighton Stuart (the U.S. ambassador, who had been the president of Yenching University when Mrs. B and I were there during the late 1920s and mid-1930s).

At the time of the Communist takeover of Nanking I began to write letters to my parents, describing events as Mrs. B and I saw or heard about them. Mrs. B was teaching an English course at the university, so had some contact with undergraduate students. Major Van Ausdall offered to carry my letters to the United States whenever he and the air attaché might be allowed to fly Ambassador Stuart out of China. These letters make up the body of this volume, dating from April 23 to July 30. I have edited them, deleting irrelevant personal material and occasionally adding bits of information from my pocket diary.[2] Although there are published firsthand accounts of the Communist takeover of

Peking and early developments there, written by Derk Bodde,[3] A. Doak Barnett[4] and others, I know of no published narration in English of events in Nanking during this period other than the brief account of the Indian ambassador, K. M. Panikkar[5] though there must be detailed reports in American and other government archives written by such able and well informed observers as Ralph Clough and Ambassador Stuart. I have therefore decided to publish these letters of a foreign witness, as uneven and fragmentary as they are, because they record what Mrs. B and I saw and heard about while living there and so may be of some use to persons interested in the beginnings of the People's Republic of China. I have found little duplication of the material in these letters in the two large volumes devoted to China in *Foreign Relations of the United State, 1949*,[6] but many similar events in Peking are mentioned by Bodde and Barnett. My letters went first to my parents in Berkeley, then to Mrs. B's sisters, and finally to colleagues at Cornell. The original letters have since been lost, but my father had had a copy typed, which I found several years ago while preparing the papers I have accumulated since I first went to China as a graduate student in 1928 for deposit in the Cornell University Archives.

Mrs. B and I found Nanking in a state of frustration and hopelessness when we arrived there on March 19. The PLA stood poised across the Yangtze awaiting a propitious moment to cross and there was little confidence in the ability of the Nationalist defense forces to stop it. The capital had earlier been abandoned by Generalissimo Chiang and the cabinet of the National Government. And inflation was out of control.[7] One occasionally heard Chinese say that the Kuomintang had "lost the Mandate of Heaven," reflecting an ancient concept regarding the inevitable fall of an incompetent government. A number blamed the United States for the Kuomintang debacle, some declaring that we should have sent in our armed forces to destroy the Communists or at least have dropped atomic bombs on them. Others complained that by giving the National Government as much help as we did we made it dependent upon our support, with the consequence that it did not make the effort it could have to overcome the obstacles and opposition that confronted it.

Many Chinese were torn trying to decide whether to remain in Nanking when the inevitable Communist takeover should occur, hoping to find acceptance under the new government, or to flee, either because they disapproved of Communism or because they feared reprisal for their connection with the National Government. One of our friends, a rather critical member of the Kuomintang, decided to leave, he told us, because he felt that his children would find better schooling and career opportunities elsewhere. Should things develop favorably in China, he said, he had a brother remaining behind who could help him establish connections should he decide to return. Even whole government agencies faced this dilemma, two interesting examples I heard about being the Institutes of Social Sciences and of History and Philology of the Academia Sinica, the first of which remained in Nanking and the second moved to Taiwan. The government agencies in control of Nanking during the month we were there before the PLA crossed the Yangtze frequently seemed confused or indecisive. For example, some student demonstrations critical of the government were dealt with very gently, presumably either because the leaders were the sons and daughters of prominent officials and military officers, or because some of the responsible officials sympathized with the students' complaints and were themselves preparing to turn over to the Communists, as some are reported to have done later.

As noted in my letters, the "liberation" of Nanking was comparatively uneventful, thanks to the hasty withdrawal of what remained of the National Government and its troops, the discipline of the PLA, and the restraint of the local population, who did relatively little looting and that confined largely to the offices and homes of departed Kuomintang officials. It naturally took some time to set up a new city administration, but the break was a relatively minor one as order was quickly restored and the necessary governmental activities were continued or soon revived. Important officials were brought in from North China. Some lesser ones came from the local underground. And it was necessary to use many former Kuomintang officials who were experienced and familiar with local conditions, subject of course to severe scrutiny. Left wing students, many of whom had run great risks organizing and demonstrating under the Kuomintang, were not employed as they had expected to be, until they had been thoroughly reeducated, and many felt frustrated and even disillusioned. It was Communist Party members scattered about the city, who had remained hidden and relatively safe before the liberation, who moved into the lower positions of authority. The best the students could do was to apply for admission to a cadre training university and subject themselves there to months of indoctrination, frequently painful questioning and criticism, and trying self-examination, before being assigned to minor government positions in a newly liberated area.

All of the important foreign embassies remained in Nanking prior to and after liberation, though the ambassador of the USSR (alone, though all had been asked) accompanied the cabinet when it moved to Canton in January. Communist officials denied the official status of these embassies and theoretically would deal with their staff members only as individuals, though this idea proved to be rather impractical and various compromises had to be made in Nanking and Peking, as even a casual look into the China volumes of *Foreign Relations of the United States, 1949* demonstrates. Some minor harassment of foreign embassy and consular officials occurred, particularly in the early stages of the liberation, such as the brief invasion of Ambassador Stuart's residence by several PLA soldiers, and some interference with movement about the city, as mentioned in my letters. I myself had no contact with any Communist officials during our stay in Nanking other than my interview with Huang Hua and my few visits to the Alien Affairs Office in pursuit of exit visas, all of which I initiated myself. Although I had several close friends in the U.S. embassy, I was in no way privy to any of its official activities. Even my call on Huang Hua to urge continuation of the exchange of students and advanced scholars between China and the United States was my own idea and I was not representing the American government, although Mr. Huang may have thought that I was sent by our embassy.

Although I do not remember very much of significance that occurred in Nanking between April 21 and August 1 that is not discussed in my letters, I do recall a couple of developments that I evidently forgot to record there and which are surely worth mentioning. Sometime in June a savings system was set up by the People's Bank of China under which money could be deposited in the form of savings units based on the current prices of rice, cloth, coal and cooking oil (as I recall). When the deposited units plus interest were withdrawn the depositor was paid the number of People's yuan required to buy an equivalent amount of those commodities if there had been any increase in their prices.[8] Chinese friends in Nanking and later in Shanghai told us how helpful this system was, making it no longer necessary to rush about changing their salaries as soon as received into illegal but stable silver dollars (stable because of the value of the silver they contained) or buying necessities that had to be stored away for later use. It should be noted, however, that although this savings system may have checked the inflation somewhat, it clearly did not stop it.

I was frequently struck during our stay, though I neglected it in my letters, by the mildness of the measures generally taken by the Communist authorities to punish violations of regulations and other misbehavior. Whether they really believed it themselves or were only trying to undermine opposition, they declared from time to time during this period that all Chinese except a handful of incorrigible class enemies were capable through reeducation of becoming acceptable citizens ("people"), and they appeared determined to appeal to the virtuous inclinations of all. The newspapers frequently published the apologies of individual wrongdoers ordered by the authorities and reports of street cleaning and other acts of public service ordered as expiation for bad behavior. If there were more severe punishments during this time, including executions which became common later, they were not announced in the Nanking press.

The U.S. embassy plane, carrying Ambassador Stuart, and my letters, left Nanking on the morning of August 2 and reached Okinawa shortly after noon. My pocket diary and my recollections suggest that our life went on thereafter much as before. The press became increasingly anti-American following the publication by the U.S. Department of State shortly after the ambassador's departure of *United States Relations with China* (the so-called China White Paper), but we detected no personal animosity among the Chinese with whom we came into contact. The Communist authorities were very much occupied with the deteriorating economic situation, which became steadily worse in spite of their best efforts, aggravated by widespread drought in the north and the devastating flooding in the Yangtze valley that is mentioned in my letters. It took a long time and great effort to reestablish the balance between production and consumption that had been upset by years of warfare, first against Japan and later between the National Government and the Communists. Some of the causes of inflation under the Nationalists continued to plague the new government even after peace was restored, in spite of the rapid rehabilitation of transportation, the virtual elimination of official corruption, and widespread appeals to the people for cooperation and increased effort.

I was worried during August by the problem of getting out of China in the face of the Nationalist blockade that kept all ships from entering Shanghai and the unwillingness of local officials to allow foreigners to go by train to Tientsin where some foreign ships were calling. However, after the American government had arranged with the two Chinese governments for the American President Line's S.S. General Gordon to visit Shanghai in September to take out Americans and other foreigners,[9] I settled down to finishing my research and preparing for our departure. I had no difficulty securing exit visas and baggage clearance, and none of the trouble with employees over dismissal payments endured by some U.S. and other government officials. We took the night train to Shanghai on September 18.

There we spent the following week completing arrangements for our departure, meeting again with old friends, and noting changes that had taken place since we were there in March.[10] Although considerably subdued, Shanghai was still much livelier than Nanking, as indeed it had been for the past century. We did some shopping and had some good meals, finding relatively little change in the stores and restaurants we visited except that prices in U.S. dollars were much higher than they had been six months earlier. We learned that the first foreigners who had come to take the S.S. General Gordon had had their baggage thoroughly examined by local officials, taking hours. But by the time we appeared the number of passengers had become too large to handle (there were more than 1,200 passengers aboard that ship, as I recall), so our baggage, which contained my collection of Nanking newspapers, was not even opened except for a briefcase full of research materials that were barely glanced at. Just as in Nanking, I found the few officials I dealt with polite and even friendly, reflecting none of the anti-American attitude that was so prominent in the press. Our ship sailed early on September 25. It was an army transport taken over by the American President Line with little evident modification and was crowded and uncomfortable, but we had a smooth passage to Hong Kong. We flew homeward from there on October 1, the day on which the local newspapers were full of the proclamation in Peking by Communist Party Chairman Mao Tse-tung of the new People's Republic of China.

The Letters

Saturday, April 23, 1949

The peace negotiations between Nationalist Vice President Li Tsung-jen and the Chinese Communists collapsed suddenly on Wednesday. That night there was heavy bombardment across the Yangtze River. Mrs. B and I were out late (after eleven!) at a dinner party near the U.S. embassy and had to come home by pedicab, which we did not enjoy and had not anticipated doing. It gave us an eerie feeling to come through the night without street lights (I do not know why the lights had been turned off), not seeing a soul except a couple of scared-looking policemen disclosed by my flashlight. Thursday night we attended a dinner at a restaurant part way down town and walked home afterward, but we came back before nine o'clock while the streets were still full of people and vehicles.

Last night we were kept awake by heavy firing along the river but had been asleep for a while when we were awakened at 5:30 by one of our neighbors who reported that the city was being evacuated by Nationalist troops and that the police had fled. It later developed that only part of the police force had disappeared. We also heard that there has been much looting of government buildings and residences today, confirmed by the fact that we have seen a lot of wood from buildings being carried along our street this afternoon—floor boards, window frames, beams, etc., and have heard buildings being torn apart not far—possibly at the Chinese air force hotel. Yesterday planes shuttled overhead all day long moving out party and government officials and others who wished to leave and could find the money for a ticket. A "last call" was issued by the U.S. embassy for all American citizens to leave who are not willing to remain under the Communists, but unless people could get away by plane it was already too late.

There have been rumors that rice and flour shops have been looted, and that the Communists already have patrols in the city that are shooting looters on sight. The men who live in this University of Nanking faculty residence compound met this afternoon and decided to patrol the compound tonight anyway; I and my group of five will be on duty from 9 to 11 pm. The Communists are scheduled to take over control of the city tomorrow morning and should restore order promptly. There is real fear here of rioting and looting. The hasty withdrawal of the Nationalist troops relieves much anxiety because the depredations of undisciplined armed soldiers are most feared, based on past experience. Local criminal elements, and even poor ordinary people, are likely to loot in the absence of authority—this is what is reported to have been going on all day in government buildings, food shops, and the deserted homes of officials who have fled, and what the university is hoping to avoid.

When I went to the university library this morning I found my research assistant, a graduate student at the National Central University, much disturbed by the rumors he had heard. We persuaded the librarian to allow him to take an armful of the books he had been using to work on at home during the next few days. I escorted him part way, through a quiet section of the city but one in which disorders had been rumored. Then I came on home myself, also laden with books. Classes were cancelled just before Mrs. B's English class was to meet, so she came home too, and we have remained in our compound since. We were to go to the Cloughs for dinner tonight but that was called off as no one wants to be traveling about in an unpoliced, or an entirely inadequately policed, city at night.

Tonight there are fires to be seen in several sections of the city, and there is a lot of seemingly aimless small arms fire—the latter presumably coming from trigger-happy residents whose motive is to frighten away robbers. There is also some artillery fire toward the south—the direction in which the Nationalist forces have retreated. Professor M. Searle Bates (a historian on the faculty of the University of Nanking), who delivered a lecture in Shanghai Thursday night and was returning to Nanking on last night's train, found himself and his train held in Chinkiang by the Communists this morning. He is still there but was allowed to phone his whereabouts.

Monday, April 25

The Voice of America radio reports that there is a news blackout from Nanking and I fear this information may be disturbing to family and friends in the United States. Actually it has been quiet here since Sunday morning. Saturday night there were numerous fires and heavy explosions about, the latter at some distance—probably magazine explosions at abandoned airfields and military bases. There was some nearby small arms fire all night, frightening to hear, but our compound patrol concluded it probably came from local guards to discourage looters and robbers. Police of some sort were on duty in the neighborhood and the street lights remained on; and we encountered no trouble. Communist troops entered the city yesterday morning and we remained in our compound all day. I went at intervals to the house of one of our neighbors where there is a telephone to pick up news and rumors. Some looting is still going on, particularly in back streets, but the arrival of the People's Liberation Army (PLA) has had a calming effect and last night was the quietest in a week. We did not renew our compound patrol and I think everyone got a good night's sleep. PLA troops are said to have marched through the city most of the day yesterday though we did not see them. We are told that it will be several days before the Communist authorities formally take over the city; meanwhile a local committee of prominent citizens exercises control.

Ralph Clough came in for a few minutes yesterday afternoon—he had driven about the city a bit and reported everything orderly wherever he had been. He said that several U.S. embassy people had managed to phone relatives in the United States Saturday night to reassure them but that his call had not got through and that by Sunday morning the long distance lines had been cut off. Everyone we are in touch with seems quite calm—in fact there is a considerable feeling of relief that serious disorder and greater destruction have not occurred. The people of Nanking have very unhappy memories of 1911, 1927 and 1937; and their old people still talk of the slaughter of 1864 when the city was taken from the Taiping rebels. So they tend to be fearful of warfare and its attendant evils. Our cook's wife has been telling Mrs. B lurid tales of the bestial treatment local people suffered from invading Japanese soldiers in 1937. It is no wonder that they feel relieved today even though they have no idea what changes in their lives the new regime will bring.

One of the most extraordinary products of times such as these is rumors. How they rise, expand, and spread! and how rapidly! We have heard many within the past few days, some of them so fantastic that one wonders how anyone could believe them. Fortunately telephones continue to function and some newspapers to appear, both of which help to discredit, but also to spread, rumors. It is amusing to hear someone swear that such and such took place because his mother-in-law or cousin saw it happen, whereas it is actually physically impossible for such a thing to have occurred.

It rained all night last night, no doubt extinguishing all remaining fires and perhaps dampening the enthusiasm of some of the looters. If it gets any cooler we'll have to light our kerosene heater again. We have had electricity throughout the "change-over," and we have running water today after none yesterday. There are several wells and cisterns in the compound, but piped in running water is a greater convenience. We are lucky to have had a cache of supplies left in the house by a former occupant whom we pay for the canned goods of various kinds—and varying quality—that we use, making it unnecessary for the cook to do much shopping during this time of unstable prices. The compound has large vegetable gardens and the cook's chickens provide us with fresh eggs, so we have been well prepared for any emergency.

Tuesday, April 26

We did not stir from the compound all day yesterday; we had little desire to do so both because of the continuing rain and because of our wish not to get involved in any "incident." Today, however, has been a beautiful day and things have gone on more or less as usual. I went to the library shortly after 8 a.m., carrying back the books I had brought home on Saturday. My research assistant was already there, having returned the books he had taken with him. We both worked on our research most of the morning, though we took a little time to discuss the changed situation. Mrs. B went to her class at 11, but only half the students were there and they were disturbed throughout the hour by other students singing and shouting in the halls—whether from joy or intent to disturb was not clear. This afternoon a contingent of University of Nanking and Ginling Women's College students, including some of the prettiest girls, marched off bearing flowers and banners to welcome the liberators. (Later we heard that their reception had been a rather cool one and that they had returned somewhat crestfallen.)

About an hour ago Mrs. B and I ventured out for the first time, with Fritz Mote, an American graduate student and Fulbright scholar, who lives with a Chinese family in our compound. We walked over to the main street, Chung-shan Lu, then down it several blocks and back home by another route. We found PLA soldiers on guard in front of the nearby bank and in front of two large buildings that had been wrecked and burned by looters Saturday night—one, the Judicial Yüan, I am told made a magnificent fire, but it was set ablaze after I came off patrol duty and had gone to bed so I didn't see it. We met a small column of garrison troops and saw a couple of patrols; they appear to be well-behaved and serious-minded soldiers but not "crack" troops.

There are still rumors of burning and looting, but I am inclined to believe that few are well-founded. All the big shops that we passed were barred and shuttered, but business seemed to be carried on as usual in some of the smaller ones. Among the men standing on street corners were some still dealing in silver dollars, exchanging one "big head"—that of Yuan Shih-k'ai—dollar for one U.S. dollar.

Mrs. B was talking with the cook's wife this morning and reports that what she—and probably many others—fear most, now that the newly arrived troops appear to be well-behaved, is change. There have been hardships and disruptions in the past but they have been adjusted to; now all is to be changed and no one knows what is to come next. The city still is under an interim local administration and I have not heard when a permanent government is to take over. The liberators are probably as astonished as everyone else at the relative ease and speed with which they have moved in and have not yet had time to draw up a government for Nanking.

Wednesday, April 27

This has been the first summer-like day since we arrived in Nanking on March 19. I worked all morning at the library and part of the afternoon, then carried home two dozen *ts'e* (Chinese type volumes) of Chang Chih-tung's Collected Works for my assistant and me to work on during the next three days while the library will be closed for the regular spring vacation. It is fortunate for the vacation to fall at this time because the students are too busy with singing, talking and other activities related to the liberation to do any school work anyway. This morning I tried to scotch a rumor spreading about the city that Dr. Stuart, the American ambassador, had fled before the Communists arrived and is with Chiang Kai-shek. I telephoned Dr. Stuart from the library and talked with him in the presence of two students, so hope that news of the untruth of this rumor will spread at least among the students of two universities.

We had a bombing this morning—at least something started a huge gasoline fire south of the city and I heard planes several times, including one that came in low and was being fired at by machine guns. Otherwise the situation continues to be quiet. We still have not taken any long walks about the city though there apparently is no good reason why we should not. There have been several minor incidents such as the invasion of Dr. Stuart's house by several PLA soldiers, the temporary seizure of the cars of one or two foreigners, and the issuance of orders to several foreigners to remain in their houses, but all have been minor—presumably the unauthorized acts of curious soldiers or "eager-beaver" cadres and are not taken very seriously.[11]

The city continues to be run by a committee of local leaders, including President Wu Yi-fang of Ginling Women's College. The

Communists, who have had almost no urban experience until very recently, must be hard put to find in their own ranks enough competent people to administer the large cities that have fallen to them. Shanghai, particularly, should present tremendous problems. We are glad that we are not in that city. I cannot believe that the disorganized and badly-led armies of the National Government will be able to hold it very long, and even while they hold it they cannot be depended upon, I fear, to keep very good order.

Professor Bates, who was stopped in Chinkiang on Saturday morning on his way home from Shanghai, is still there. A telephone message from him yesterday said the local Communist authorities refuse to recognize the validity of the National Government visa on his passport. The university has sent a letter identifying him and asking that he be allowed to return to his post in the university, where he is badly needed. In Chinkiang he is staying at a Christian mission school and reportedly is allowed the freedom of the city. I expect we shall all run into this visa problem ultimately as the Communists may try to use us to secure recognition by the U.S. government. However, so long as they allow me to carry on my research, and to leave the country before the end of July, I personally shall have no cause for complaint.

We shall be glad when we can receive mail again. It is a strange feeling to be cut off from the rest of the world, though we are not, really, as long as we are allowed to listen to the BBC and the Voice of America and have electricity to do so.

Thursday, April 28

It is much cooler today and looks like it might rain again. We hope it will rain and stop the bombing. A Nationalist B-24 circled overhead for two hours this morning dropping bombs in Hsiakuan, the suburb to the north on the bank of the Yangtze where the Nanking railway station is located. It evidently was aiming at the electric power plant upon which the city depends for electricity and indirectly for running water. We are naturally glad the bombs missed their target though we are sorry that a number of innocent people were killed and injured where the bombs did strike. Such bombing does not endear the National Government to the people of Nanking it has deserted.

The U.S. embassy chancery and a number of adjoining residences were put under close guard this morning by the PLA with the result that the Cloughs and other Americans living there are confined to quarters. This was done two days ago at Ambassador Stuart's residence and other embassy residences adjoining his, and foreigners in other embassies and in some missionary compounds have been similarly restricted—all "for their own protection." So far it has been possible to move freely about the neighborhood in which the University of Nanking is located, which is away from main city streets. This is not an unexpected development and is not expected to last long—only until the local political situation is clarified. A new Nanking military government was set up this morning under the chairmanship of Liu Po-ch'eng, the famous one-eyed Communist general. Presumably it will remain in control until a new civil government can be established, which may be some time unless the National Government's resistance in the Shanghai-Hangchow region collapses very soon.

This morning Mrs. B and I went over to call on the two "war widows" living in our neighborhood: Mrs. Bates, whose husband is still in Chinkiang, and Mrs. Gelwicks, wife of the assistant U.S. military attaché, who is living with three small children in a house not far from here and whose husband was cut off from Nanking in Wuhu but managed to get to Shanghai. I hope nothing is done to interrupt the local telephone service for it means much to isolated people like Mrs. Gelwicks, and we also are happy to be able to communicate with friends elsewhere in the city. There is no phone in our house, but there is one nearby in the same compound and one in the university library where I work. I learned today that a friend managed yesterday to send a telegram for us to our families reassuring them regarding our safety.

Local prices are behaving crazily; the shopkeepers don't know what to charge, so charge plenty. I was charged two or three times what I should have been for a haircut yesterday but since I paid only the equivalent of 25 cents U.S. I cannot very well complain. Today's newspapers report that the barbers' union presented cokes (cakes?) to PLA soldiers yesterday so perhaps I was contributing to the cause. We are buying as little as possible these days, eating from our reserve supply of canned goods, which are not very tasty, being mostly army stores left over from the war, but nonetheless meet our needs.

Sunday morning, May 1

We have just had our usual Sunday morning breakfast of hot cakes, which are one of the specialties of our cook, another being *chiao-tzu*. With the hot cakes we could have either orange marmalade, blackberry jam or karo syrup—the last two from our own supply of canned goods, the first obtained from a neighbor in exchange for a jar of peanut butter. We have enough canned tomato juice on hand to last us, we hope, until fresh fruit is available. We also ate some Australian sausage, though not much can be said for its taste, perhaps because it has been in a can too long.

Friday and Saturday were so cold again that we had to relight our kerosene stove. The heavy rain Friday and low-hanging clouds yesterday kept the bombers away, but they are overhead this morning, evidently trying again to knock out the electric power plant. Our life continues to be very quiet—almost dull for what people in the USA might expect to be exciting times. I suppose there would have been things to see had we felt free to wander about the city during the past week, but not knowing the temper of the liberator we have not wanted to risk stirring up any latent anti-foreignism. Several foreigners who were out on the streets have been told by PLA soldiers to go home and stay there, but others have wandered about freely without incident. Those who have been out have reported little that was unusual so we evidently have not missed much. Yesterday we did miss a display of *yang-ko* dancing put on at the university athletic field by PLA soldiers. Unfortunately we did not learn about it until late and arrived just as the exhibition was ending.

The new order is gradually establishing itself, although the shortage of personnel is quite evident. The Communists really have a job on their hands to administer all the big cities they are taking over. Our only knowledge of the military advance of the PLA comes from the one-sided local newspapers and the Voice of America—which is also one-sided in the other direction, its reporters having access only to the censored reports of Nationalist commanders, However, I suspect that the PLA is meeting with very little resistance, since there was no real resistance to the crossing of the Yangtze—the most formidable natural barrier in this area. We hear stories—mostly unauthenticated but probably having some element of truth—of a battalion or a regiment of well equipped Nationalist troops surrendering without even a pretense of resistance. Now there is another B-17 in sight; it appears to be bucking heavy winds, which will make bombing even more erratic than usual. And more innocent civilians will be killed for the benefit of Generalissimo Chiang's "face." Even if the power plant is knocked out the harm will have been done to the people of Nanking rather than to the advancing PLA.

I have collected a few newspapers to take back to Cornell. I have all copies of the formerly influential Catholic newspaper *I-shih pao* from April 22 until today. A *Chieh-fang hsin-wen* (*Liberation News*) appeared two or three times during the past week, but yesterday it was absorbed into the new *Hsin-hua jih-pao* (*New China Daily*) which is presumably to be the official newspaper in Nanking. It is well printed on good paper and is much larger than any other newspapers—as was the old official *Chung-yang jih-pao* (*Central Daily*) before its demise a week ago today. Various newspapers have issued a few numbers and then disappeared. Of those published under the old regime only the *I-shih pao* and two or three "mosquito" papers have continued to appear, possibly brought out by completely new personnel, certainly under different editorial control. Other papers I have seen during the past week are the *Ch'ien-chin pao* (*Advance Newspaper*), the *Chung-ta jen-pao* (*Central University People's Newspaper*) and the *Chung-kuo jih-pao* (*China Daily*).

All kinds of organizing and reorganizing is going on, to meet the challenge of the new order. Laborers, merchants, students, teachers, all are being organized for the first time or reorganized by enthusiasts who have long been so inclined or have just jumped onto the bandwagon. I have an impression that a relatively small group of politically-minded students are actively agitating and organizing and that the less politically-minded majority tag along, no doubt fearful of being accused of an unbecoming lack of enthusiasm for the new order. There are supposed to be big demonstrations today—May Day. It will be interesting to see whether the students return to class tomorrow. There is much talk of reorganizing the universities—re-adjusting salary scales, changing the curricula, etc.—but such things are still in the talking stage.

New currency regulations have been proclaimed with an exchange rate of one *jen-min yuan* (People's dollar) for 2500 "gold" yuan (National Government dollars) on Friday and 2800 gold yuan on Saturday. The pre-liberation black market in silver dollars still exists. Someone bought twelve "big head" silver dollars yesterday with a U.S. $10 note, and our cook got over a million gold yuan for one "big head." When the banks open tomorrow we may find that a rate of exchange in People's yuan has been set for U.S. dollars. I hope so, as the exchange rate in the black market under the former government was very unpredictable.

That bomber overhead just dropped two bombs over toward Hsiakuan, evidently still aiming at the electric power plant. Today's paper says that fifteen children and two laborers were killed in the Thursday bombing and more than twenty persons were injured. The latest report is that today's large May Day demonstration has been postponed until tomorrow, for fear of strafing by Nationalist planes.

Sunday night, May 1

Here are a couple of authentic episodes: Friday morning George L. Harris and others were being driven to the USEFC (United States Educational Foundation in China) office when their car was stopped by a half dozen PLA soldiers who ordered them out at bayonet point, meanwhile scolding them for riding in a car instead of walking, and abusing the Chinese driver for working for foreigners. George explained that it was an office car, that they did not mind walking but had received no instructions from the new government regarding such matters. The soldiers were persuaded to allow the car to go on to the office empty and to permit the erstwhile riders to proceed on foot. PLA soldiers appear to be under no specific orders regarding their behavior toward foreigners; once in a while someone runs into a nasty one, but on the whole they have acted civilly. However one never knows what to expect or what is expected of him. Today, for example, I am told there are no PLA guards at the U.S. embassy gates, whereas two days ago the gates were so closely guarded that no foreigner could get in or out. When there are guards the same man is never in the same place twice, and each buck private apparently is left to handle the situation as he thinks fit. Until there is a bit more direction Mrs. B and I plan not to wander very far from home.

Another episode: Yesterday at the *yang-ko* dance staged by PLA soldiers on the University of Nanking athletic field, the French photographer Henri Cartier-Bresson asked if he might take some pictures and someone gave him permission. But when he had shot his roll some soldiers came to him and demanded that he surrender the film, saying they did not want foreigners to see pictures of the liberation army. Cartier-Bresson hung onto his camera—not understanding Chinese so not knowing what the fuss was about except that bayonets were pointed at his throat—while he urged his interpreter to explain. But the soldiers shoved the interpreter aside and seized and broke the camera. A number of the students there, though unquestionably sympathetic toward the liberation, indicated that they thought the foreigner was being unfairly treated, and someone even murmured the old saying about the unreasonableness of soldiers no matter what army they belong to. All this took place before we got there, but I have the facts from a reliable eyewitness who understands Chinese.

Professor Bates is still in Chinkiang, though he has been able to get two letters to Mrs. Bates, carried by Chinese who either walked to Nanking or came by truck. He reports that he thinks he has persuaded the authorities to let him return to Nanking and expects to catch a ride on a truck soon. He has had no trouble in Chinkiang other than being kept there, but has found it hard to locate those in authority.

Tuesday, May 3

A follow-up on the Cartier-Bresson episode: His camera was returned to him Sunday, evidently not badly damaged, with an apology. Then yesterday he visited the University of Nanking and formally thanked its students for helping him at the time of the incident. The May Day demonstration has been postponed again, until tomorrow— May 4 being a holiday celebrating the May 4, 1919 incident anyway. I have heard no reason for this new postponement; perhaps the authorities still fear Nationalist planes, though none has appeared today and the one yesterday did not stay around long.

The students are all back in classes this week and the situation at the University of Nanking appears to be normal—except for the problem of meeting payrolls and other expenses. The university keeps its funds in U.S. dollars and the banks are not yet changing foreign currency into People's yuan, in fact exchange rates have not yet been set. The money problem is also serious for private individuals like us whose cash is in U.S. dollars. We have been exchanging—or rather, our cook has been exchanging for us—a dollar at a time on the street, but the dealers have become afraid to accept U.S. dollars for fear an arbitrary exchange rate may be set that will cause them to lose money. Those of us who had not put away silver dollars have been on the spot the last day or two; we, for example, have not been able to pay our servants' wages for the second half of April and we are without money to buy food. So we have been eating from our reserve of canned supplies and some vegetables from the compound; and yesterday the cook killed and prepared for us one of his chickens. Today I was able to borrow thirty "big head" silver dollars from the USEFC which I hope will carry us until we can exchange U.S. dollars again. There is no logical explanation why the Yuan Shih-k'ai "big head" dollar is exchanged on the black market for 20-25% more than the Sun Yat-sen "small head" dollar which, I am told, contains at least as much silver as the "big head."

I understand that President Ch'en Yu-kuang of the University of Nanking was told last night by the highest officials of the city that continued receipt by the university of contributions from private American sources would be encouraged. It is only U.S. government funds that are not wanted. This last reflects a point frequently emphasized by the Chinese Communists: that the Chiang Kai-shek government was able to carry on only with foreign aid and was ultimately weakened by such dependence, whereas the Communists intend that China shall depend upon itself alone even if recovery and progress are delayed thereby.

This morning Mrs. B and I walked over the USEFC office with Fritz Mote, to pick up the silver dollars we were borrowing there. We saw several groups of PLA soldiers, but they paid us no attention. Bud Harris reported that there are not only no PLA guards at the embassy today but that he had come by car to the office without interference. Some local Chinese "in the know" say that the placing of PLA guards at the various foreign embassies was really intended, as claimed, to protect them, that the Communists had been fearful of incidents that might be provoked by a Kuomintang underground. This strikes me as credible, and not negated by the cases of soldiers entering foreign houses—notably that of Ambassador Stuart, ordering foreigners to remain at home, and even seizing their cars. Such cases may be explained by the absence of specific orders from above, leaving individual soldiers to "play by ear," or by the inevitable presence in such a body as the PLA of overzealous and antiforeign individuals. Actually there is a marked lack of emphasis on anti-Americanism and antiforeignism in general in the proclamations, slogans, etc. that I have seen since the liberation.

We hear reports that Shanghai is having a bad time at the hands of its defenders. Yesterday the radio reported that the big hotels had been occupied by Nationalist soldiers. An explanation heard here is that although civil leaders in Shanghai had offered the military a thousand gold bars to withdraw their soldiers from the city the military were demanding ten thousand and were allowing their soldiers to damage valuable property to exert pressure. I am told that no one here expects the Nationalists to put up any more of a defense of Shanghai than they did of the Yangtze crossings.

Thursday, May 5

We are going to have lunch with Major Van Ausdall (assistant U.S. air attaché) tomorrow and will take these accumulated letters to leave with him, on the theory that he will be one of the first to leave—though there is no expectation that the embassy plane will be flying out very soon. He came by with a form cable blank yesterday on which we indicated which message was to be sent to our families. We picked the one that said we are fine and that mail is not coming through.

We walked over to the Clough's this afternoon—the first time we have been there in two weeks and our second venture away from the university neighborhood during that time. There were many green-yellow uniformed soldiers to be seen between here and there, most of them apparently quartered in the fine houses left vacant by departed Nationalist officials, but none paid us any attention. There is no PLA guard at the embassy and embassy people are driving their cars once more. Members of the new regime can hardly criticize foreigners for riding in cars, as some did at the beginning, for they themselves are now riding about in jeeps and cars.

We did not see the liberators march into Nanking but persons who did report that the first column consisted of ex-Nationalist soldiers who had surrendered near Hsüchow several months ago and were still wearing their gray uniforms, but with armbands indicating that they now belong to the PLA. The first PLA troops stationed in the city included a lot of country-yokel types and a number of stories are now circulating about them. One tells of a family approached by soldiers quartered next door who asked how to open the electric light bulb in a table lamp so it could be lighted with a match. Shown how to turn on the electric switch the soldiers were delighted; in fact members of the family saw lights flashing on and off most of the night. And when the soldiers were moved on southward they cut the wires and carried the table lamp with them. I am told that the quality of the soldiers being moved through Nanking has improved during the last week, and we have heard of no new incidents. During the first week there were some stories, a few from fairly reliable sources, of soldiers demanding rice and fuel even from some poor people, but I have not been able to check on their truth. Certainly we have heard a great many rumors during the past two or three weeks that later proved to be false.

Today was the last day for the legal exchange of the National Government's currency for the new People's currency, at the rate of 8000 "gold" yuan for one People's yuan, and hereafter the former will not be acceptable. Unfortunately the new currency is also showing signs of weakness; in fact its exchange value in silver dollars broke badly on the black market yesterday and today. The rate four or five days ago was 400 People's yuan for one "big head"; yesterday morning it was 430, this morning our cook got 500, and I hear that it went to over 600 this afternoon. It is a pity, for nothing would boost the morale of the people of Nanking quite as much as the achievement of stability in the purchasing power of their money. So far the new currency has no more solid backing than the old—it is all printing press money. But it is expected that the new government will be much readier to clamp down on speculators than the old, and to make a serious effort to grapple with the money problem. Local officials are clearly worried about this problem and have asked the university to help with the calculation of a cost-of-living index.

Friday, May 6

The People's currency went above 700 to the silver dollar for a while this morning but dropped to 600 this afternoon. These are of course black market figures; I have so far heard of no official exchange rate quoted for silver dollars. The explanation of yesterday's rapid rise appears to be that the Nanking city employees who have remained on the job were all paid an advance of 2000 People's yuan and promptly rushed out and bought silver dollars with it, continuing the well-established local custom of converting paper money into hard cash as soon as possible and also deflating the value of the People's currency. It is also said that PLA soldiers have been buying silver with their pay. Whether this is generally true or not, it is reliably reported that the soldiers passing through Nanking have bought all the flashlights, fountain pens, and rubber soled shoes that were for sale in the city and the shopkeepers who sold them have not doubt put much of the paper money paid for these things into silver dollars. There is no market for U.S. dollars but fortunately we now have enough silver dollars to meet ordinary expenses for awhile.

Some of our American diplomatic acquaintances have had little to do since the liberation and are beginning to find life rather dull. A sort of social life is beginning again for them, but foreigners still avoid going out in the evening. We ourselves have seen relatively little of people not connected with the university—almost nothing of non-university Chinese. Fortunately I have been able to carry on my research work, and Mrs. B's English class is meeting again after some irregularity. Today we had an interesting lunch with Major Van Ausdall, Col. John A. Dunning (U.S. Air Attaché), and Henry Lieberman of the *New York Times*. We tried to piece together some of our impressions, but it is still too soon after the change in government, and we have access to too little information, for us to draw any but the most tentative conclusions about what is going on. We miss the foreigner-owned Shanghai newspapers, which although they publish a certain amount of unconfirmed rumor still contain a lot of dependable news. Our local newspapers—I have now settled on the *New China Daily*—contain almost no news, being filled largely with doctrinal articles, new regulations, announcements of the commendable activities of patriotic labor, student and other groups, and the political biographies of Communist leaders. The little news that appears evidently is selected for a definite political purpose. Almost the only foreign news I have seen in local newspapers since the Communists took over control had to do with a leftist International Conference meeting in Paris to which the Chinese Communist Party sent delegates, and an announcement that the American Committee for a Democratic Far Eastern Policy had been declared a subversive organization by the Attorney-General. The U.S. Information Service here still distributes an English-language news bulletin, and we listen to short-wave newscasts, but if these are denied us, which is not impossible, we shall be shut off from news of the outside world. Even the little news we hear about Shanghai comes to us via these foreign broadcasts.

One more bit of information about the Cartier-Bresson episode: His camera was returned to him by the same half dozen soldiers who had taken it from him. They apologized profusely, saying that their commanding officer had scolded them for their stupidity and had explained to them that only the photographing of fortifications and other military objects is forbidden, a category into which *yang-ko* dancing could not possibly be fitted.

Sunday, May 8

It has been a beautiful day—hot but not muggy; and the past two nights have been brightly lighted by a full moon. We have been out twice during the past two days besides our regular trips to the nearby campus. Yesterday afternoon we attended a Home Economics Department tea at Ginling Women's College, which was the largest gathering we have been in since the liberation. Today we walked to the Clough's and had a picnic lunch with them in the garden of the Diplomatic Club next to the U.S. embassy. We are eating quite well these days, including lettuce from our compound garden and green peas and strawberries from the university gardens. This is the first time we have lived anywhere in China where we could get lettuce and strawberries that had been grown under conditions that made them safe to eat uncooked.

We have heard stories of "underground railways" by which Chinese are still getting away to Shanghai and to South China. One group of arrangers is said to guarantee for 200 silver dollars to take a person safely to Shanghai—going first to Soochow by bus, then by canal boat the rest of the way. There evidently is no fighting in that region, despite Nationalist claims, and the Communists presumably have no objection to Chinese going. There is also a regular bus route open to Hangchow, from which the passengers go by various means to Ningpo and on to South China. I have heard that a full bus load of people left yesterday. Foreigners still are not allowed to travel. Professor Bates is still in Chinkiang, where he was stopped more than two weeks ago. Transportation has been restored but the officials in charge there have not allowed him to leave.

The Communists are being very hard-boiled in their attitude toward foreign governments, most of which, including that of the United

States, they do not recognize. I ran into this before Nanking was liberated when I mailed a letter to a friend in Peking addressed to him at the American consulate-general. It passed across the lines readily enough, but was returned stamped with the statement that no such place was known there. In Nanking a rudimentary foreign affairs office has been set up with Huang Hua in charge, but it deals with foreigners as individuals and refuses to recognize the existence of the embassies as such. A formal request presented to that office by an American officer was not even read because it was written on embassy stationery; he was told that a request written on plain paper and signed by him as an individual would be considered. A protest against the occupation of an empty embassy house by PLA soldiers, made on grounds of international law, was not accepted though read, but the bearer was told that the occupation was a mistake, that no foreign property in Nanking was to be occupied by troops, and the soldiers were quickly withdrawn.

I was told today that the reason Nanking fell so suddenly was that the Nationalist division that was holding Pukow, just across the Yangtze, or its commander, was bought by the Communists. Also that the Wuhu defence collapsed when a captain, whose company held a crucial position, sold it to the PLA for twelve silver dollars. It is generally accepted that many Communist victories were facilitated by the bribery of Nationalist officers and that quite a bit of the American equipment the PLA now possesses was bought rather than captured from Nationalists. It is also generally believed here that there has been relatively little actual fighting on this side of the Yangtze and that Shanghai will be taken with little or no fighting whenever the Communists feel ready to occupy it.

Yesterday I asked a prestigious and well-informed Chinese (President Wu Yi-fang of Ginling Women's College)[12] for an explanation of the clearly much less enthusiastic reception of the liberators in Nanking than in Peking. I was given several reasons: As to the students' attitude, they had received many letters during the previous three months from friends in the north informing them that life under the new regime was not all they had hoped, that students there were getting very small food allowances and that there remain many restrictions on their freedom. Another factor was the briefness of the siege of Nanking— Peking was under fire for some time, food, fuel and electricity were scarce, and a strict curfew was enforced by the Nationalists there, with the result that there was a great sense of relief when the city fell. Nanking, in contrast, was occupied quickly and easily and no great tension was created to be relieved by the arrival of the PLA. Another factor was the historic unpopularity of the Kuomintang in Peking, from which the national capital was removed in 1928. Modern Nanking, on the other hand, was built largely by the Nationalists and a large portion of its population depended directly or indirectly on the National Government for a livelihood. There was consequently much less anti-Kuomintang feeling here than in the north. Whatever the causes, the liberators have not been received here with any marked degree of enthusiasm. The huge demonstration originally scheduled for May Day and postponed to May 4 has not been held and I have seen no satisfactory explanation.

Tuesday, May 10

I am writing this by candle light as we are without electricity, for the third night. We are told that the coal supply is low at the power plant and that although there is plenty of coal, already mined, not far away in Anhwei province, a bridge that is out between there and here will delay renewal of Nanking's supply. What electricity there is is reserved to pump water for the city's system—a wise choice, in our opinion. Nanking introduced daylight saving time last Saturday, to save electricity. Where we miss electricity most, when it is off, is for the radio and the electric iron.

The post office has begun to accept ordinary letters (no air mail) addressed to the United States—presumably to be sent via Tientsin and Hong Kong, so we have mailed several, hoping they will go through. Since the mail service to Peking is said to be fast we have written to friends there. It is still true, as it has been for half a century, that the Chinese Post Office is an extraordinarily efficient organization, getting the mail through in spite of wars, natural disasters and changes of government.

Wednesday, May 11

We have electricity tonight, for a change, but since it has already been off once it may not last the evening. And the new daylight saving time will be discontinued tomorrow, with no explanation other than that Peking has decided against it and that Nanking will follow Peking.

It is my impression that the transition from Kuomintang to Communist regime is proceeding with relative speed and smoothness, and there appears to have been a minimum of upset for much of the local population. Their earlier experiences in Peking and Tientsin obviously have been helpful to the liberators, not only enabling them to avoid many pitfalls here but also supplying them with ready-made regulations and patterns of organization and action. They appear to be quite sensible in dealing with local problems: protecting both public and private property—except that of former officials who have fled; encouraging the reopening of stores, factories and schools; trying to stabilize prices; and preventing the abuse of citizens and their property by soldiers.

One of the most striking developments has been the slapping down of the small group of radical students who apparently had decided that they were going to run the university, abolishing examinations, compulsory class attendance, and other onerous burdens. Yesterday morning an elderly Communist educator from Yenan lectured the University of Nanking students for two hours. He said, among other things, that of course regular class attendance and examinations are necessary and that the students should settle down to study and work hard at it. He said that even though teachers may have oppressed students in the past there is no excuse for students to oppress their teachers. He urged them to treat Americans well, saying that the American people are friendly to the new China, it is only their Wall Street-controlled government that is against it. He is reported to have explained one interesting thing about the new People's currency—that it is based on rice and that only as much has been issued as can be backed up by the current rice harvest. Naturally this can only be estimated, but it does seem to mean that the authorities do not intend to print unlimited amounts of paper currency, as the Nationalist Government did. Actually the black market rate for People's yuan in silver dollars has been fairly steady the past few days. The new professional salary schedule for Peking has been published in the local newspapers. It is based on millet, and presumably will have to be translated into rice for this part of the country. But local wage earners and salaried persons are beginning to get some idea of how much they are going to have to live on—or how little.

When I talked by phone with Ralph Clough today he reported that the Nanking Alien Control Office had informed him that certain regulations concerning foreigners are being issued: There is a curfew between 11 pm and 5 am; no foreigner may go outside the city wall without a special permit; foreigners may not wear military uniforms; and foreigners with cars must reregister them but may continue to drive during the reregistration process. Otherwise foreigners are presumably free to move about as they will. As soon as we can exchange U.S. dollars again—and that is now promised within a few days—we shall be back to "normal." Incidentally, Professor Bates has returned home from Chinkiang, but I have not yet had an opportunity to talk with him.

A rumor has spread about the city to the effect that Chiang Kai-shek and his troops will march back into Nanking on May 15 without firing a shot, the PLA presumably having already fled across the Yangtze. This has been foretold by a famous soothsayer at the Four Corners downtown whose prophesies during the Japanese occupation always proved to be correct.

Sunday, May 15

Well, Generalissimo Chiang and his troops failed to arrive today; presumably the army is too busy running in the other direction. We are told that the PLA is approaching the Fukien boundary. Life for foreigners in Nanking has become relatively "normal" once more, with some revival of social activity, though Mrs. B and I have so far gone out only during the daylight hours. There has even been electricity all the time since the 11th.

I become increasingly impressed with the closeness of the intellectual—and perhaps emotional—ties between the Chinese Communists and the USSR. During the past week the local press has reprinted a number of articles attacking American imperialism in one or another of its real or imagined manifestations. These articles follow the same line, even use much the same language, as Russian attacks on the United States during the past two or three years. Moreover the foreign news in the *New China Daily* comes almost exclusively from Tass or the Polish News Agency, distorting it to a remarkable degree. For example, an article today on the lifting of the Berlin blockade tells how the USSR has steadfastly promoted peace since the defeat of Germany, in the face of constant provocation by the war-mongering USA and its satellites Great Britain and France. Another article attacks the Indonesian leaders in the current U.N.-sponsored negotiations with Holland as having sold out their fellow Indonesians and all other native peoples in Southeast Asia to the United States. The *New China Daily* has made much of Henry Wallace's testimony against the North Atlantic Treaty; and it has expressed sympathy for the Ford workers in America who suffer from the "speed-up," while on the same page there is an article praising Nanking automobile repair workers for having adopted a new slogan: "Repair more! Repair better! Repair faster!" The paper has also made much of the reported increase in size of the American Communist Party by 800 members.

During the past three days I have put in a good many hours at the U.S. embassy with the assistance of copyists from the University of Nanking Library making copies of a list of about 800 books published in Manchuria and China during the past three years by the Chinese Communists. The books were purchased by the U.S. consulate in Dairen early this year for the Library of Congress and I have been permitted to make copies of the embassy's list for Cornell University and for the University of Nanking Library, which is trying to build up a collection of Chinese Communist publications. To me the most interesting fact revealed by the list is the large number of items about the Soviet Union and/or translated from Russian. There is now no doubt in my mind that the Chinese Communists really look to the USSR as their best friend and source of inspiration, and that they intend to indoctrinate the Chinese people with their attitude; and I think U.S. policy toward China will have to take this into consideration. I doubt that the Chinese people, in view of their long experience with Russian relations, can easily be persuaded that unquestioning support of the USSR is always in China's interest; but shutting them off from all but slanted information should make it easier to secure their acquiescence. It will be interesting to see whether the authorities carry out their reported threat to prevent all short-wave radio listening; also whether they allow such a "friendly" American publication as the *China Weekly Review* to continue publication after they occupy Shanghai.

There has been much said in the local press this past week about a National Youth Conference that has been meeting in Peking. Today a list of permanent committeemen was published and I was surprised to see among the "youths" two Yenching University professors, Yen Ching-yüeh and Weng Tu-chien, who must be at least as old as I am, Huang Hua (who graduated from Yenching in the mid-1930's), and several people I knew in Chungking who will certainly never see 35 again.

The foreign exchange situation is still in a muddle. Peking was queried about it recently by a local official and the reply stated that facilities for the exchange of U.S. dollars and an official rate are to be established as soon as possible but that personnel competent to manage them are not yet available. Meanwhile foreigners in Nanking are buying silver dollars with U.S. dollars on the black market at a rate of approximately one for one, then buying People's yuan with the silver dollars. Several days ago silver dollars converted to only 480 People's yuan, but the price went back up to 550 today. It is anticipated, based on the rate now in force in North China, that U.S. dollars will exchange here officially for about 1000 People's yuan, and that once a U.S. dollar exchange rate is set officially the silver dollar will buy between 400 and 500 People's yuan. But this is no more than guessing.

Tuesday, May 17

Well the exchange situation has been settled. A proclamation was issued yesterday forbidding all further transactions in other than People's notes and one other type of Communist note, and stipulating that gold bars, silver dollars, and foreign currencies may be exchanged hereafter only at government banks. The rates fixed yesterday were 530 People's yuan for one "big head" silver dollar and 545 People's yuan for one U.S. dollar. When some person complained that the rate in the north is more than 800 yuan for a U.S. dollar and about twice that for a silver dollar a responsible official responded that each section of the country is expected to fix the rules to suit its own situation. Such a low rate will be particularly hard on the University of Nanking and Ginling Women's College, which depend for a substantial part of their income on funds coming from abroad. I have an idea that no foreigner will exchange any more money than absolutely necessary at that rate and that the black market will continue to flourish—at least until a few operators have been shot as examples. I am told that a sudden change in the black market rate on silver dollars about ten days ago is thought to have been due largely to the execution of some operators in Wuhu.

The new regime appears to be making a sharp distinction between former government officials who ran away before the liberation and those who remained in Nanking. I heard today of a group of Kuomintang officials who had planned to flee but only half of whom managed to get away. The half that were caught by the swift change, in trying to make the best of the situation, asked to be allowed to carry on their old jobs under the new management. They were not only warmly welcomed but each was given a 2000 People's yuan bonus—or perhaps it was an advance on salary. The other half got only as far as Chinkiang, which was occupied before Nanking was, where they were caught in some crossfire and several members of their families were killed, so they returned to Nanking. Learning that their fellows were occupying their old positions, they applied for reinstatement but were categorically rejected. I have not heard whether their homes were taken over by the new government as were those of other higher officials who ran away. I suspect that the Communists will be very reluctant to re-admit the many officials and other members of the upper class who fled before them, should they wish to return. However they may have to make exceptions of technicians and other professionals, particularly if these had not been active politically. The new regime certainly faces an enormous task in the running of this huge badly damaged and poverty-stricken country and will probably have to accept any competent assistants who are willing to cooperate on its terms.

Radio reports we heard tonight—Voice of America from San Francisco and U.S. Armed Forces short wave from Los Angeles—indicate that Shanghai is about to be occupied by the PLA. The sooner the better, say I, as it is inevitable; and life must have been very frightening there during the past two weeks.

Friday, May 20

Today we paid our first visit since liberation to the nearby branch bank and exchanged a U.S. $5 bill. The rate has been raised slightly twice since the first announcement and today we got 580 People's yuan for each U.S. dollar; silver dollars were bringing only 520. (I dealt with the same short, slender bank teller who had changed money for me under the old regime, but now a large, rather bewildered looking PLA soldier sat on each side of him, either because he is not completely trusted or to enable them to learn how to be bank tellers.) We then walked down to Taiping Road where I bought a few books at the Commercial Press. The part of the city we saw appears to be fairly normal; most shops are open though not much business is being done. Most of the people with money are believed to have fled and those remaining are not flaunting it. Prices appear to be pretty stable; some, such as those on important staples like rice and flour, have declined slightly during the past week.

I think the Communists have done a remarkable job in the taking over of this city. They have moved quickly and efficiently to deal with the essentials: police protection, electricity and water, food supplies, prices, public health, and transportation. There has been a lot of pious propaganda, but the necessary jobs have been done. The local people, who have seen a number of changes in government, seem unable to get over their astonishment at the efficiency of the administration, the evident good will and conscientiousness of individual officials, and the excellent behavior of the soldiers. A missionary with whom I have talked said that the discipline of the soldiers has impressed him most— they are ignorant country boys like most other Chinese soldiers, yet their leaders have imbued them with something different. He has seen many armies come and go but this is the first time in his memory when there have not even been rumors of abuse of the local population.

The director of the Central Hospital is reported to have said at a Rotary Club meeting that conditions in his institution are better than they were for the past couple of years under the National Government. During the period before liberation he had had a terrible time securing the money from the government needed by the hospital; he had had to pull all kinds of wires and resort to various tricks just to keep it in operation. Now two administrative officers are assigned to the hospital, who, so far at least, have devoted themselves to providing liaison with the city government. When the director needs anything he puts it up to these two officers, who take it to the top city officials and come back promptly with a decision. One small incident he related had to do with PLA officers stationed nearby who brought their soiled clothes to the hospital to be laundered. The director explained to the liaison officers the hospital's incapacity to serve as a laundry for outsiders and they promptly obtained an order from the city government instructing the PLA to do its own washing.

The Communist officials assigned to govern Nanking have run into many problems they had not encountered before, and although they can lean on regulations and precedents already worked out in Peking and Tientsin they are frequently baffled by their own ignorance and inexperience. The University of Nanking, desperate for funds—it had to skip a pay-day today—has been trying to cash a good-sized check drawn on New York. But the officials running the People's Bank do not know how to handle such a transaction. Today they phoned the university treasurer and asked what they could do with such a check if they did cash it. However the new people learn quickly, and do not seem afraid to ask questions about matters they do not understand, in contrast to the attitude of most old-fashioned Chinese. The Communists are assuming tremendous responsibilities, but if one can judge by what we have seen so far in Nanking, they are likely to succeed in their undertakings. Some people say that the situation in Tsinan was as hopeful as it is here immediately after its liberation but that before the end of the year it got "very bad," and that the conciliatory period is already drawing to a close elsewhere in the north. I have no way of knowing how reliable such statements are.

A member of the Russian embassy staff told a U.S. embassy officer the other day of an incident in which one of the Russian wives, in labor, was being rushed in an embassy car to the hospital during curfew time. The car was stopped by PLA soldiers and compelled to return to the embassy for a pass or an interpreter. The Russian relating the incident then asked if the U.S. embassy had met with any such unpleasant treatment from the liberators and appeared quite disappointed when the answer was negative. The American apparently forgot to mention the episode in which PLA soldiers invaded the home of the American ambassador.

Monday, May 23

The defense of Shanghai evidently has been more vigorous than was expected by people here; at any rate the few reports that trickle through suggest that there has been some severe fighting.

Today I visited an exhibit of historical materials relating to various student incidents from May 4, 1919 to April 1, 1949 which have been collected by the Nanking Student Union—mainly by history students at the Central University, the University of Nanking, and Ginling Women's College, I am told. It was quite interesting, consisting mainly of relevant contemporary newspaper, magazine and pamphlet materials. Large posters gave brief histories of the various incidents, usually managing to show a connection with American imperialism; and there were some photographs, banners with slogans, and the remnants of some bloodstained clothing. Prominently displayed were two large new banners, one detailing the stages of American aggression in China during the past two or three years, the other listing the "new Twenty-one Demands" of American imperialism. I wonder how many of those who helped prepare the exhibit were aware that many of the leaders of the May 4th and June 23rd incidents which they have spotlighted are at present among the "enemies of the revolution," some even on the Communists' list of "war criminals." The exhibit was shown at the Central University on two days last week, at the University of Nanking yesterday and today, and will move to Ginling tomorrow. I was not in a position to observe yesterday, but all day today a stream of people has poured through, mostly students of all ages. Many were brought from their schools in trucks and buses, others marched in columns, singing and sweating—it has been a hot day.

Yesterday, being Sunday, I abstained from historical research and read the local "news"-paper almost all the way through. Much of it is too dull to read every day, full of reports of meetings of student groups, labor unions, etc., and of long, repetitious articles of exhortation. By reading through most of yesterday's paper I was impressed once more with the meagerness of the intellectual fare being provided those who live under the Chinese Communist regime and with the onesidedness of the little news that is printed. Yesterday a long speech made in Harbin by Kuo Mo-jo upon his return from the Communist "Peace Conference" in Paris was printed in full. It is shocking to see that that great scholar has become a demagogue. He did not really tell anything about the conference except the complimentary things that delegates from other countries said about Mao Tse-tung and the Communist cause in China; and he elaborated on the fine impression Russian, Czech and other reception committees had made on him as he traveled through their countries, and he described the May Day parade in Red Square, Moscow.

Most of the foreign news, as I have noted before, is from Tass or the Polish News Agency, and all of it follows the current Russian line without perceptible deviation. I was amused to read in a speech made by a Chinese educator a statement that China must eliminate all foreign influence from its educational system and rebuild it upon the Marx-Engels-Lenin-Stalin line. At another meeting a Chinese economist acquaintance of mine who has just returned from two years in the United States is quoted to have declared that Chinese intellectuals must now study as a guide the actions of Russian intellectuals at the time of the Russian Revolution. Unless my memory is at fault he seems to be advocating something resembling suicide. A Chinese friend to whom I showed a USIS quotation of Secretary of State Acheson's statement that the United States is not working for a Pacific Pact was baffled that he had seen in the *New China Daily* the flat statement that the American government *is* working for one. As he commented, "Someone must be lying."

Wednesday, May 25

Reports of the Communist occupation of Shanghai this morning appear to have been confirmed. It will be interesting to learn the real facts about the fight for that city. There is a feeling of relief in Nanking, not only among those who have relatives there, but also among those who have been feeling that the economic situation here would remain in suspense until Shanghai was liberated and once more back in operation. The reopening of foreign communications also had to await the taking of Shanghai; now we shall see how long the Communists will take before readmitting foreign ships and planes. They probably have not enough trusted and competent personnel to move very rapidly, and they may not be in a hurry anyway.

We are going to Major Van Ausdall's for a cocktail party later this afternoon and I shall take a second installment of these letters to add to those already in his care.

Saturday, May 28

On Thursday I called at the Alien Affairs Office,[13] requesting an interview with Huang Hua, the director, to inquire about the intentions of the new regime with respect to the exchange of Chinese and American students and research scholars. Mr. Huang recognized my name—we had flown to Peking together in General Marshall's plane in February 1946, and he accorded me a cordial welcome and a pleasant interview. We talked in Chinese—with a stenographer busily taking notes—and I am afraid that I did not present the case as well as I could have in English. I told him of the number of American scholars currently in China and of others now preparing in American universities to come to China for additional study or research; and I reminded him of the many Chinese who have studied in American colleges and universities. I then asked him whether he could give me any idea, before my departure for the United States, of what his governments attitude may be regarding such a two-way exchange, so that I might pass along the information to interested universities after my return home. He replied that no decision had yet been made regarding such an exchange, that such a decision would have to be made at a high level, and that the pressure of other more urgent matters would prevent consideration of such a policy in the near future. However, he said that he would pass along my request that the exchange of students between the United States and China be allowed to continue.

A friend who is unusually knowing about things Chinese believes that the atmosphere of Chinese-American relations in the immediate future will depend upon the outcome of the current foreign ministers' conference in Paris: that if the conference closes in a harmonious spirit the new Chinese government—when it is set up—may be expected to be at least civil, if not friendly, toward the United States; but that if a new break occurs between the USSR and the Western powers the atmosphere in China is likely to become decidedly anti-Anglo-Saxon, with any exchange of Chinese and American students out of the question. I am afraid that Chinese Communist suspicion of the United States is so strong that such a research project as a village study carried out in a Chinese village by an American scholar will not be permitted, for some time to come anyway. In the course of a friendly conversation with Huang Hua a week or two ago, Henry Lieberman of the *New York Times* said he would like to go to a Communist-controlled village to observe the actual operation of the much-talked-about land policy, but Huang replied that that would be impossible. It appears pretty certain that Americans are not to have the same opportunity in the foreseeable future to observe the phenomenon of Chinese revolutionary change that they have enjoyed in the past.

I am astonished by the readiness with which many Chinese allow themselves to be taken in by the Russians. Ambassador Stuart told me recently of a conversation he had had with a Yenching University graduate who had returned from Manchuria full of enthusiasm for the program of Russian economic exploitation there. Dr. Stuart asked him what difference he could see between present Russian and previous Japanese activities there, to which he replied that Japan had had greedy, nationalistic purposes whereas the USSR is acting solely in the interests of the Chinese people. I expect that the Chinese, even the Communists, are in for a shock some day when they realize what the Russians really are up to there. Come that day they will doubtless lay the blame on the United Sates because of the Yalta agreement; and I must admit that I think our government deserves blame for that giveaway. In time I think the Chinese will wake up, for they are not stupid—only hypnotized by the Russians and resentful of American support for Chiang Kai-shek and his government. Russian representatives may not be pleasant to deal with but Russian propaganda has evoked an enthusiastic response among the Chinese.

We have had a good deal of social life during the past week. Life in Nanking had become so dull that even the foreign ambassadors have taken to consorting with mere professors. We have welcomed invitations from them as our life, too, has become less interesting since we are seeing fewer Chinese than before the liberation. Some of our Chinese acquaintances left with the National government; others who remained are reticent about being seen with American imperialists. My work goes on as before but I think we shall feel ready to leave when the time comes. We are learning quite a bit about the Chinese Communists from their newspaper, but though of interest it, too, makes pretty dull reading. We remain very grateful for the Voice of America news broadcasts and the mimeographed news sheet issued by the Nanking office of the U.S. Information Service. Without them we would have no idea of what is going on in the outside world.

Monday, May 30

Our first American mail since Nanking's liberation was delivered yesterday, evidently brought on the first train to leave Shanghai after that city fell to the Communists, which arrived yesterday morning. It had accumulated in Shanghai after connections with Nanking were cut. Now we shall have to await the reopening of communications between Shanghai and foreign ports for the reestablishment of normal overseas mail service.

Friday, June 3

We expect external communications to be reestablished soon because the new regime has expressed a desire for prompt revival of the pre-liberation pattern of foreign trade. All reports suggest that normal operations were restored in Shanghai more quickly than in Nanking, in the face of much greater problems. Besides having had the earlier experience of taking control of Nanking the authorities were better prepared in other ways to take over Shanghai. They are reported to have delayed occupying Shanghai while they assembled the personnel needed to govern that city, collected a large quantity of People's yuan notes, and made other necessary preparations, in nearby Soochow. In any event they moved in quickly when they did move and Shanghai is now reported to be in pretty good shape. There is considerable comment among local Chinese regarding the apparently increasing "liberalism" of the Communists as they have moved southward. There is no doubt that they learn quickly and that they realistically face the fact that they cannot effect radical changes at once with the small number of trusted personnel available to administer the huge territory they have suddenly secured control of. They may now be merely securing their position, with consolidation and radical changes to come later. As far as I have been able to hear or observe they place only their own people in key positions.

Some of the local pro-Communist liberals, not a few with proven ability, are unhappy to find themselves completely ignored by the Communists. They retain their positions if they are in universities or similar institutions, but they are not consulted by the new governmental authorities. I understand that the local universities are still in turmoil as students and workmen struggle with the faculty for control of curricula, financial administration, etc., and competing cliques in each category quarrel among themselves over matters both important and trivial. Students—at least certain elements among them—are said to urge changes running all the way from modification of course requirements and methods of teaching to the abolition of some departments. There have been some bitter attacks on individual members of university faculties—some of them doubtless deserved.

I have commented to several Chinese acquaintances on the fierceness of the attacks on the United States in the local press. Most, perhaps over-optimistically, consider that such attacks are intended only to help win popular support for the new government—are only propaganda. They say that in private conversation Chinese Communists attack only the imperialistic United States government and deny any antagonism toward the American people. They are very "proper" in their dealings with foreigners, as far as I can tell. They still make much of not formally recognizing the existence of foreign embassies and consulates; for example, the motor cars belonging to the U.S. embassy must be registered in the names of individual members of the embassy staff. But that pretense is difficult to maintain and may not last long.

Wednesday, June 8, 6 pm

It looks as if the Communists have run into economic difficulties in Shanghai. Prices on commodities have been rising rapidly here during the past few days and the People's currency seems to be in real trouble as people flee from it into silver dollars. A week ago silver dollars were being sold for as little as 600 People's yuan—less than 100 above the official rate. On Sunday Fritz Mote got 1060 for silver dollars in the licensed black market, and I got about the same for US dollars—with reports of considerably higher rates in Soochow and Shanghai. On Monday the local People's Bank raised the official rate on U.S. dollars from 580 to 760 and on silver dollars from 520 to 720, but the black market broke loose this afternoon with silver dollars buying as many as 1600 People's yuan and U.S. dollars trailing a bit behind. Meanwhile commodity prices have doubled and trebled as people rush to invest the People's currency they receive in food and other useful things. Of course the situation here largely reflects the gigantic Shanghai market. The Communists are going to have to act fast or their currency will follow the course of the currency issued by the National Government, which can bring satisfaction to no one except perhaps the corrupt incompetents of the previous regime. The people of Nanking—and probably of the other liberated Chinese cities—have been skeptical of the stability of the People's currency from the beginning, but they certainly will not be pleased to have their fears realized. One wishes that the Communists had had more experience with the complexities of urban economics before taking on Shanghai, because neither the doctrine of dialectical materialism nor their extensive rural experience is likely to be very helpful in such a situation. It will be instructive to see how they cope. I do not expect them to throw up their hands and allow matters to take their own course as was the usual practice of their predecessors.

The *New China Daily* today printed the eighth and last installment of a vicious attack on Hsiao Chu'n—who also writes under the name of T'ien Chu'n—known to Americans through the publication of a translation of his *Village in August*. Hsiao, a native of Manchuria and still, or at least until recently, a person of great influence in literary circles there, fought the Japanese with Communist guerrillas in the early 1930s, then was an important Communist writer in Shanghai for some time, spent eight years in Yenan, and returned to Manchuria after the Japanese surrender where he is reported to have published an influential journal in Harbin. He is being criticized for disapproving of the civil war as a fratricidal struggle, and not trusting Russian motives. The article, which evidently aims to destroy him, attacks his writings in detail, quoting out of context and calling him such names as "selfish individualist," "petit bourgeois," "feudal bureaucratic capitalist," and "against the principles of Marx-Lenin-Mao." It is puzzling that this long article should be published here at this time, for it appears to be intended to intimidate non-Communist intellectuals at a time when the Party is seeking the support of such intellectuals. It certainly serves as a warning to Communist writers not to depart from the official line. It is surprising that so much that Hsiao has written is quoted in the article, for not a few readers who were not already familiar with Hsiao's writings are likely to feel sympathetic toward his views.

We have just heard that Ambassador Stuart is leaving for Shanghai Saturday night. It has not yet been announced, but we suspect that he is on his way to Washington—possibly on the S.S. President Wilson that is due in Shanghai and scheduled to sail for the United States on the 15th. He will depart after a wedding and a big reception at the Ambassador's house on Saturday afternoon to which most of the American community is invited. Henry Lieberman of the New York Times is marrying Kay Martin, Dr. Stuart's secretary.

Same night, June 8, 10.30 pm

The Bates and the Cloughs were here for dinner tonight and Professor Bates had some interesting information concerning local Communist tactics. Surprisingly the real directors of some Communist activities still have not made themselves known. For example, in the current pressure for reorganization of the University of Nanking, which comes from a student group with some cooperation from instructors and assistants, most of the real operators remain behind the scene. This Communist student group was well organized and ready to act when liberation took place, demanding the immediate reorganization of the university into five equal groups: (1) professors and assistant professors, (2) lecturers (instructors?) (3) assistants, (4) students, and (5) workmen. They talked about revising the curriculum and other things, too, but time has shown that they are primarily concerned with securing power, with getting rid of the regular university administration and putting their own people in control. In the beginning the student group tried to execute a coup by securing acceptance of a new constitution and organization without discussion, but the faculty balked this effort and arguments have been going on now for more than a month. Like the Communists who infiltrated American organizations, these Chinese Communists depend upon disciplined organization, smoke screens, the wearing out of opposition by protracted discussion, and playing off one group against another to achieve their ends. The Communist student group may win in the end, if it can secure government aid, but the non-Communist faculty and students are learning a lot about their tactics and are beginning to fight them with their own weapons.

Professor Bates also told of a meeting of Nanking educators last week. It was rigged in such a way that the tone was set by the first few speeches, which were made by selected persons. Following these everyone else present was called upon to speak even though the meeting dragged on for hours. After all had spoken the chairman, clearly not an amateur in such proceedings, gave a masterly summary of the meeting in such a way as to reinforce the points he wanted to make, often using the words of other speakers but twisting them to suit his purpose. The press reports of the meeting also set forth certain ideas, quoting skillfully and even misquoting in some cases.

The Chinese Communists clearly are very clever at organizing and at propaganda, but the real test they face is whether they can solve the tremendous economic problems that confront them. Organization and even persuasiveness will help, but they will not be enough, in my opinion.

Monday, June 13

The Nanking authorities have taken energetic measures to put a stop to the rise in prices and to the depreciation of the People's currency in terms of silver and U.S. dollars. A number of new regulations have been issued including one raising the official exchange rate for silver and U.S. dollars, and one cancelling the temporary licenses of street exchange peddlers. The local press has been printing decrees, explanations and admonitions for three days, and at least for the moment the inflation appears to have been stemmed. The regulations look fair enough and rumor has it that they are being enforced firmly but with fairness and scrupulous honesty. This is one place where the present regime has it all over its predecessor, which is said hardly ever to have enforced its decrees fairly or honestly. Commodity prices have dropped somewhat from the high point of last week, though they remain two or three times as high as they were two weeks ago. I understand that the currency black market is now quite hard to locate and that black market rates today are not far above the official bank exchange rate.

A footnote on Professor Bates' report on University of Nanking politics, summarized on June 8: To everyone's surprise the Communist student group's pressure for reorganizing the university administration suddenly collapsed—presumably on instructions from the local authorities. In a way the faculty feels somewhat let down, though greatly relieved. It appears that student agitation is meeting with no greater encouragement from the new regime than it did from the old—certainly a surprise to the students.

Today at a friend's home we met Dr. Yao Keh-fan, the Superintendent of the Nanking Central Hospital, two of whose stories I had heard secondhand and recorded on May 20. Besides being an authority on public health and an able hospital administrator, Dr. Yao is considered one of this city's leading citizens, is the president of the Nanking Rotary Club—which is still meeting regularly though reduced in number—and is a charming and intelligent person. He reported his growing respect for the local Communist authorities under—or with—whom he is working. When he found that they evidently were pleased with his administration of the Nanking Central Hospital, demonstrated by their finding cash for his use whenever it was needed, he drew up a plan for the reorganization and integration of the hospital and public health system of the entire city, which they accepted in principle and are now working with him on the details. He feels that their strength lies in their honesty, their desire to learn, and their willingness to accept criticism. He finds that they are not afraid to confess mistakes and try hard not to repeat them. They tell him that they expect some of their people to backslide—particularly in the presence of the fleshpots of the big modern cities—but that they intend to be constantly on the alert to avoid corruption and mismanagement. If a man of Dr. Yao's character, outlook and position can continue to work harmoniously with them, I should think that almost any conscientious Chinese who is devoted to improving the welfare of the people can get along with them. It remains to be seen, however, whether they remain as flexible as they seem to be at present, in this area anyway.

Dr. Yao told one of the classic stories of the solution of a class conflict by the Chinese Communists. It seems that the unskilled help in the Lester Institute Hospital in Shanghai went on strike the day after the liberation of that city. In accord with their conception of the new order they demanded pay and food equal to that earned by doctors and nurses. The superintendent, finding the hospital's employees unwilling to listen to reason, called on the new authorities for assistance. They sent a representative who immediately called a meeting of the entire hospital staff, both professional and unskilled. The latter were asked to state their grievances, whereupon their representatives said they wanted higher pay because they worked just as hard as any of the professionals. Also they wanted a vacation because of the extra hard work they had performed during the previous few weeks. The Communist mediator acknowledged that they had worked very hard and gave them the next day off to rest, saying that the professional staff would do their work as well as its own. The doctors, nurses and technicians had no alternative but to prepare and serve meals, clean floors, empty slops, and do the other work of the nonprofessional workers of the hospital staff all the next day. The following morning when the unskilled workers returned to the hospital they were immediately called together by the Communist mediator, who told them that since they had had the previous day off he was giving the professional staff a day off, too, and that the nonprofessional workers were to carry on just as the professional staff had the day before, that is to carry out the responsibilities of both groups. They were immediately filled with consternation, recognizing their inability to assume professional duties, and begged the mediator not to ask this of them. The Communist mediator departed from the hospital, no doubt in search of other knotty problems to solve, and the superintendent thereafter heard no more complaints about unequal treatment.

The Nationalists, and perhaps the Japanese invaders before them, maintained a public address system in the old Imperial drum tower close by the University of Nanking which announced the time every half hour from 7 am to 10 pm. The propaganda department of the People's Government presumably considered such a mechanism wasted on mere time telling. It still announces the time every hour, but in between for several hours each day it blares forth speeches, patriotic songs, proclamations, and now and again even old-fashioned Chinese operas. Confusion is compounded when the university's public address system emits the amplified singing of a coloratura soprano or tones of a string quartet at the same time.

Sunday, June 19

The propaganda corps appears to be working under high pressure these days. During the drive against the use of silver dollars last week parades of slogan-shouting young people were seen on all the main streets every day; and truckloads of propagandists or little groups on foot sang songs and shouted slogans admonishing everyone to consider the unfortunate effects of the continued use of silver dollars on prices, on the farmers, and on China's new democracy generally, urging all to use only People's notes. That drive seems to have terminated, but the propagandists continue to be active on other topics. The drum tower public address system has been connected with loud speakers in other parts of the city, adding to the din.

Reports drifting in from various rural areas suggest that local Communist authorities are cracking down on Christian churches and schools in many places, particularly those run by Catholics. The commonest procedure, we hear, is to levy taxes that are so heavy that they cannot possibly be met, forcing the church or school to cease using the buildings. Although nothing of this kind has been reported yet in this city, the University of Nanking authorities are worried by the possibility. It certainly is a clever means of putting an end to the private operation of schools, hospitals and churches if the government wishes to do that, I doubt that any general policy has yet been laid down; the cases we have heard about have apparently been the arbitrary acts of local officials. Undoubtedly the Chinese Communists will eventually circumscribe the activities of foreign missionaries, who are looked upon as propagandists spreading a doctrine that is inimical to communism and, in many cases, as spies for the imperialistic American government.

There are reports of severe drought in North China and of growing unrest among the common people in many places. The food shortage in Shanghai is said to be serious since the importation of foreign rice has ceased. It looks as though the new government is in for a major economic crisis this summer, in the rural areas where its strength has lain heretofore, and in the cities upon whose labor force it would like to build its national power. The reports of the growth of resistance movements—including those of a strong anticommunist army under General Chin Keng—may be exaggerated or even wholly false, but there is no question of the reality of drought, flood and poor distribution of the necessities of life.

Several days ago the people of Nanking were told in an article in the *New China Daily* that only a few of them are productive, that the large majority have been living off government and officials, and that they must change their ways and become productive citizens. This is easy to say but difficult to do much about because there are very few factories here and not the means to build and operate them. I am told that many of the people of Nanking are actually in a pretty bad way now that the government upon which they were dependent has fled. It is quite depressing to walk, as we did yesterday, along a street lined with big stores stocked with modern Western-style furniture. Clearly none of these stores has made a sale since the end of April and probably not many since the first big exodus of people in or connected with the National Government last fall. What is more, furniture of this kind will never sell as long as the present government, with its austere standard of living for officials, remains in power. A person who left Nanking before the liberation would hardly believe his eyes if he were able to see the quiet streets of the city now; there are almost no cars, few trucks, and even very few pedicabs. Shops are open for the most part and a wide variety of wares is on display; but there is not much buying. The only really busy shop I have seen is the Communist Book Store, which is jammed with shabbily dressed people of all ages buying large numbers of books and pamphlets, which are sold to them at prices I should think are higher than they can afford to pay. High profits are forbidden for individuals, but they appear to be proper for a government agency.

Monday, June 20

Henry Lieberman, who is writing an article on the Chinese Revolution for the *New York Times Magazine*, has been pumping various foreigners here for ideas. Today he had three of us Americans to lunch at the Embassy Club with Dr. K. M. Panikkar, the Indian ambassador, who is a brilliant fellow and loves to put his ideas into words. By the end of two hours some interesting ideas had emerged, one of them relating to differences between the 20th century Chinese Revolution and earlier revolts and dynastic changes. In earlier changes of government the ruling house collapsed and was replaced by another, presumably ruling better, but within the same ideological, social and political framework. In the 20th century not only did the Ch'ing dynasty collapse, but the impact of Western culture undermined confidence in the traditional pattern, making it impossible for a Yuan Shih-kai or a Chiang Kai-shek, clinging to the old or a somewhat modernized version of the old framework, to win widespread support. The Communists, besides providing new leadership, also supply a new cultural pattern which inspires widespread confidence in them. More than that, their ideology and program are sufficiently dynamic to encourage many people to devote their lives to "the cause."

The most revolutionary aspect of the Chinese Communist movement is its expression of confidence in the common people and its extension to them of actual participation in the government. Dr. Panikkar feels that since there is no competing ideology—no strong religion—in China, Communism may catch on more quickly and enjoy wider acceptance than in Catholic or Islamic countries, or even in India where it will have to work hard to substitute loyalty to itself for loyalty too long established and highly regarded religious ideas. The group felt that world Communism will be distinctly modified by China's becoming a Communist state. With the Soviet Union no longer the sole major Communist state, no longer need the interests of world Communism be confused with those of Russian nationalism. China, even greater in population than the USSR, may in time break the Soviet Union's domination of world Communism, with the result that Communism, like Capitalism, may become a truly international phenomenon. Dr. Panikkar feels, as do Lieberman and I, that Chinese Communism has a good chance of succeeding where warlords and the Kuomintang failed, that drastic measures will be required to solve the overwhelming economic problems but that in time they will be worked out. We all agreed that it is too soon to know even what direction Chinese Communist policy is likely to take, much too soon to anticipate the nature of its successes or failures.

One member of our luncheon group feels that the old culture still has great influence and that Communism cannot offer an acceptable substitute over a long period. Two of them fear that the Chinese Communists will follow the same course as the Taipings and the Kuomintang, becoming soft and corrupt, and weak. I recognize this danger, but feel that the chances are against such Communist failure. They are not building either on the backward-looking gentry, on ignorant and corrupt military politicians, or on the spineless and directionless modern educated class—who, in my opinion, have let China and their own ideals down. They are building on the people, and they have a logical and at the same time dynamic pattern of operation. Being human beings, they may become corrupt, but they recognize the danger and are taking practical measures to prevent it. To retain power permanently they must give the people reason for wanting them to continue to lead. However, I think they are prepared to use force to remain in control if everything else fails.

There is talk that the National Government plans to blockade Shanghai, which if it materializes could cut us off even from Hong Kong and, incidentally, delay our departure beyond the July 15 date we have set. We understand that the Nationalists have also threatened to renew air bombing of Shanghai and Nanking—the last measure of moral bankruptcy, in my opinion.

Tuesday, June 21

According to the Voice of America and BBC, the National Government—still located at Canton—has declared the coast of China above Foochow under blockade commencing June 26. In advance of that date Nationalist planes have badly damaged a British ship off Woosung (near Shanghai).

I talked this afternoon with a Chinese professor (S. T. Wang) who impresses me as thoughtful, frank, and as well informed as it is possible to be in the present situation. He is a Christian, friendly toward Englishmen and Americans, and fairly openminded regarding the new regime. I asked him what he thinks the American policy should be toward Communist China. He favors non-interference in Chinese affairs, feeling that our activities during the past two or three years have done China more harm than good. He pointed out that the loose and sometimes evil behavior of American soldiers in China during and after the Japanese war had prepared the common people to believe almost anything bad they might hear about the United States. He feels that nationalism is strong among the Communist leaders, as well as among the rank and file of the Chinese people, that neither Russian nor American influences are likely to dominate China. He believes that the USSR may turn the Chinese people, including the Communists, against it by its imperialistic activities in Manchuria, and that the Communists will have to seek economic and technical aid from the United States because they will not be able to get it from Russia. Professor Wang shares the current uncertainty of many Chinese intellectuals regarding the security of their position and the possibility of carrying on impartial teaching and research. The educated class, to which he belongs and which has held a strong position in Chinese society for more than 2000 years, he pointed out, does not control the Communist Party though some members exercise some influence there.

Monday, June 27

Several days ago I went to the Alien Affairs Office to present a letter requesting exit visas for Mrs. B and me. I was told that no procedure for granting exit visas had yet been worked out but that if I would submit a sheet of paper supplying a variety of information including passport number, reason for departure, and amount of baggage, my application would be considered in due time. Permits for Nanking foreigners to go to Shanghai, and even to go to Shanghai and return, are relatively easy to obtain, but it still is not possible for a foreigner in Shanghai to secure permission to come to Nanking.

Yesterday I received a letter from Fei Hsiao-t'ung[14] in Peking answering my inquiry whether Bill Skinner could study with him at Tsinghua University. His answer was very friendly but advised against Bill's trying to get there for the present. I also received a very optimistic letter from Lucius Porter (China-born professor of philosophy) at Yenching University. He reported that Yenching (another foreign-supported university, located in a Peking suburb) seems, for the present at least, to be enjoying great favor. It is very difficult here, at least, to judge from the scattered information that comes to one just what the attitude of the authorities is toward a particular university, or toward foreigners and their various activities.

Thursday, June 30

We have done a good deal of entertaining and being entertained during the past two weeks as the time for our departure supposedly draws near. We have given three dinners at our favorite restaurant, the T'ung-ch'ing Lou, two for mostly American friends, and one yesterday, which was a rousing success, primarily for Chinese friends and Fritz Mote, our neighbor and good companion. I have been a major supporter of T'ung-ch'ing Lou since it reopened, for the new authorities do not encourage fancy eating and no one but a foreign imperialist would run the risk of social criticism by entertaining there. The restaurant's chef seemed challenged by the occasion yesterday, for he provided us with a wonderful dinner. And it was not expensive either, by American standards, for the feast for twelve people, plus three bottles of Bamboo Leaf Green wine, one tin of Capstan cigarettes and a large tip cost only a shade over US$10 altogether.

During this recent period, as I have been winding up my research and the time approaches for us to leave, we have seen two Chinese movies, visited the Fu-tzu Miao Fair area, had good meals with friends either in their homes or at restaurants, and generally enjoyed ourselves in spite of almost continuous rain. Visits to numerous old book stores have been disappointing and I have found few books that I wanted to take home with me. But we feel that we have gotten a great deal from our stay in Nanking and are now ready to leave, hoping that our departure will not be too long delayed.

Sunday morning, July 3

Air raid sirens have been screaming this morning and there was the sound of a plane overhead. It turned out to be a pamphlet raid, with many falling around our house, warning of the Nationalists' intention to bomb banks, factories, railroads, power plants, etc., "indiscriminately and night and day." Also copies of speeches by Chiang Kai-shek, Li Tsung-jen and other Kuomintang figures were dropped. We have heard that the bombing in Shanghai last Wednesday took many lives even though one of the planes dumped its load of bombs into a graveyard. Some local Britishers feel that the Nationalists may have little trouble enforcing their blockade, even though it is not a strict blockade under international law, in spite of American and British protests. I have been counting on the British to send some ships into Shanghai in spite of the declared blockade.

One does not like to take too much stock in rumors, yet the stories of exorbitant taxes and requisitions that continue to come in from liberated rural areas, and even from cities like Chinkiang, Wuhu and Pengpu, make one feel that there must be some factual basis for them. One gets the impression that the greatest care is being taken by the Communists in the larger cities, that the smaller the community the poorer the officials assigned to it. Also that there has been a definite shift from dependence on the farmer to emphasis on the urban laborer. In his July 1 speech ("On the People's Democratic Dictatorship"), Mao declared that under the New Democracy laborers, farmers, small capitalists and national capitalists will all cooperate under the leadership of labor and the Communist Party. If one can judge from the local press, urban labor is now being flattered and encouraged, possibly even at the expense of the farm population.

Certainly the rehabilitation of China and its development as a major power requires substantial industrialization, but it is difficult to see how this can be carried through successfully without the support of the great masses of land-bound farmers. The reports of farmers refusing to plant crops for fear that most of the harvest will be taken from them by the authorities must be very disquieting to the Communist high command, particularly in view of widespread drought and flood conditions, the shortage of transportation, and the seeming impossibility of importing food from abroad to meet the needs of such a great city as Shanghai.[15]

The liberators are up against problems far surpassing in magnitude and complexity any they have encountered prior to this time. No matter how good their intentions or how sincere their desire to learn, leaving final administrative decisions to country yokels, who reject the recommendations of experienced specialists who worked under the previous regime, can lead only to inefficiency and waste effort. There is a good example in the local rice situation, where in the presence of a growing shortage prices have been leaping up. There is said to be much rice rotting in warehouses simply because officials from the north sealed it when they came in and have not yet unsealed it, not realizing that in this hot, moist climate rice spoils very quickly unless it is turned over and sunned every few days.

Wednesday, July 6

Major Van Ausdall told me at the Ambassador's Fourth of July party that the embassy plane is almost in shape to fly again and that they expect to take off "sometime between now and the end of the month." We ourselves had originally planned to leave Nanking on our way home on the 15th, but now don't know when we shall be able to get away. It looks pretty unpromising at the present writing, in the presence of the "blockade" by the Chiang government. Nevertheless we took our applications for exit visas to the Alien Affairs Office this morning.

Thursday, July 7

Today the new regime is putting on the biggest demonstration Nanking has seen since its liberation—in commemoration of the outbreak of the Sino-Japanese War in 1937. But the celebration has been turned into a gigantic anti-American imperialism demonstration, with all propaganda instruments mobilized to make it a success. I have heard that at a large planning meeting on July 4th the officials in charge of the local program explained that imperialism was to be the target, that it was not to be directed against individual foreigners. Our friends, however, advised us to stay at home today, so we missed the big parade, which thanks to heavy rainclouds, was not endangered by Nationalist planes. The "Marco Polo Bridge incident" (July 7, 1937) was given an anti-American twist by attacking the alleged American rebuilding of the Japanese war machine. Today's *New China Daily* is double its normal size and crammed full of articles about the American rebuilding of Japan. The tendency in this case, as in all matters of foreign relations, appears to be to follow the Soviet Russian line. For example, the United States is charged with refusing to allow a peace treaty to be drawn up with Japan, ignoring the fact that we have expressed our willingness to enter into such negotiations providing all countries that fought Japan are allowed to participate as equals, whereas the Russians insist that the treaty be taken up at the Big Four foreign ministers' conference that represents only the United States, the USSR, China and Great Britain. The occasion has also been used today to attack the United States for other things such as the Marshall Plan, the North Atlantic Pact, and other pet USSR hates. The *Nanking Min-pao* (*People's Paper*), which appeared today for the first time, besides most of the above mentioned items launched several attacks on the U.S. itself.

Professor Andrew Roy (of the University of Nanking faculty) was reporting today some of the statements made at a recent National Christian Council board meeting by Y. T. Wu, a former YMCA secretary who was one of the Chinese delegates at the Communist "World Peace Conference" in Prague and Paris this spring.[16] Mr. Wu reported his conclusions after discussion of Christian affairs with some of the top officials in Peking. He said that the Chinese Communists look upon Catholics as reactionaries and do not feel friendly toward them. But because they consider that the Protestants are doing socially useful work they will be encouraged to carry on. He asked, if this were the case, why a number of Protestant churches had been closed or their work interrupted in other ways. The reply was that such acts were against orders, but that many local officials had been inadequately indoctrinated, that they often look upon Christian activities as imperialistic because of their foreign connections or that they associate them with local superstitions that the Communists are trying to eliminate. And sometimes they consider that church buildings are insufficiently used, or could be put to more socially significant use. When Mr. Wu asked whether the authorities would be willing to issue new instructions in line with this friendly attitude, the reply was that this would do Christians more harm than good because following general Communist principles they would have to present arguments against as well as in favor of religion and the former might then be used by enemies of Christianity as an excuse to increase anti-Christian activity. The best way to handle the situation, he was told, would be to submit specific information regarding abuses to the authorities, who would then act secretly through the party machinery. Mr. Wu stated that he is now gathering such information.

Mr. Wu says that Communist officials have declared that they will not interfere with missionary institutions like Yenching University for several years, but that he doubts their willingness to allow such influential educational institutions to operate as they wish for that long. The Communists seem to encourage continued operation of missionary hospitals, though there is some doubt regarding the continuation of religious work in connection with them. Foreigners will continue to be welcome, but only as workers. None will be allowed to serve in a policy-making or administrative capacity. The principle set forth, according to Mr. Wu, is that foreigners such as missionaries, educators, and technicians who can be of service to the Chinese people will be both needed and welcomed, whereas foreign business men may be needed but not welcomed—whatever that may mean. Continued financial support from foreign non-governmental sources probably will be permitted, although that has not been specifically stated (except by some officials in Nanking).

Friday, July 15

We had hoped to be leaving China by today, but that proved to be expecting too much. We have toyed with the idea of going north, but were told that foreigners are still unable to take a ship out of Tientsin. So far Nanking weather has been unusually cool for summer; this house is well located and well arranged for hot weather anyway. I am beginning to worry about the danger of not getting back to Ithaca in time for the fall opening of Cornell. There seem to have been some unexpected obstacles placed in the way of the departure of Ambassador Stuart, although we saw the embassy plane completing its test flight yesterday.

A full American statement of the Olive case was published yesterday by the United States Information Service in an attempt to counteract the misinformation that has appeared in the Chinese press. This was the first overt anti-foreign action in this area but it should not have been a complete surprise in view of the constant stream of anti-American propaganda.[17] The case demonstrates that there is at present no assurance of protection of foreigners under the new government, and it gives a reason for the speedy recognition of the Communist regime—which would provide our government with means to protect its citizens, at least with the machinery to protest arbitrary actions and mistreatment of Americans.

The economic situation continues to deteriorate, drought and flood, as well as the Nationalist blockade, contributing to an already bad situation. Not much had been said in the local press about the floods that we have heard for weeks are very bad, but the authorities finally made a clean breast of the situation on the 13th, admitting that this year's floods are more severe than any since the terrible floods of 1931. The

Yangtze River is still somewhat below previous high marks here, but the newspapers report that all previous marks have been topped at Anking and Kiukiang upstream. Fortunately our two-week-long rainfall stopped a few days ago so the danger of severe flooding in Nanking may have passed. Some parts of the city are under water now, but that evidently is an annual event.

Even more serious than flooded houses are flooded rice and cotton fields. Various figures on the extent of damage to the rice crop are bandied about, the only sure fact being that it is serious. I understand that the cotton crop at the university's experimental farm, which ordinarily pays the overhead on all its farming operations, is a complete failure. Prices continue to go up and even the vegetable crops were severely damaged by the long period of rain. In the two weeks before July 13 the commodity price index used by the People's Bank of China for its savings deposit system rose 87% as a result of which the bank reported it had lost about 50 million People's yuan. Meanwhile there are reports that this deposit system, which was intended to preserve the purchasing power of all money deposited and seemed a very sensible method, is being curtailed somewhat. The Communists continue to be plagued by their economic inexperience and by their unwillingness to act on the advice of the non-Communist experts they consult.

Today I bought twenty gallons of kerosene for 48,000 yuan, about US$26.00.

Thursday, July 21

Ambassador Stuart and the embassy plane are still here. The most obvious explanation is the demand by local authorities for "shop guarantees" for the people who will accompany the ambassador: pilots, mechanics, and perhaps a few embassy personnel. This is an outrageous demand, for what Chinese business man is going to stick his neck out voluntarily in times like these by guaranteeing an American, especially one connected with the U.S. government? The embassy position is that such a requirement for diplomatic and consular personnel is unacceptable under international law, Dr. Stuart may also feel that the Olive case demonstrates that Americans are not safe in liberated China at this moment and that he should remain here until the situation improves.

We are being bombed again. The local press reports that two Nationalist planes took two lives and injured more than twenty persons on Tuesday; and it sounded as though a plane that flew over yesterday also dropped bombs, though I am not sure.

Sunday, July 24

If one can judge from the press, and from current rice prices here and in Shanghai, the disturbing general price rise of a week ago has been checked and there has even been a decline, at least in the all-important price of rice. The authorities evidently have made valiant efforts to move rice and other necessities into the large cities, with some success. Local people say that rice prices ordinarily are highest at this time of year—just before the harvest, but that speculators begin to unload their remaining stores as harvest time approaches, gradually lowering prices. If this holds true this year, the peak may be passed, helping the authorities to hold down the price level. It is costing us considerably more to live than it did six weeks ago, for whereas prices have gone up from 100 to 200 percent during that time the exchange value of the U.S. dollar has been increased by only one-third. Since wages and salaries are supposed to be based on the price of rice, it is not difficult to understand the jam the University of Nanking finds itself in, depending as it does so largely on funds from the United States. Henry Lieberman reports from Shanghai that all costs for foreigners have jumped drastically there, that he and Kay have been paying around US$10 per day each for food at the American Club, which is about three times what we paid there in mid-March.

Perhaps as the aftermath of the typhoon on the coast last Sunday and Monday we have had several days of unusually nice weather. Nanking had high winds and high water but nothing to compare with Shanghai, which was very badly hit. We have also had three days without an air raid and were beginning to hope that the Nationalist air force was busy with the war, but today we have had three alarms though no planes have appeared yet.

Last night at dinner at the Harrises we had an interesting conversation with a Miss Liu, a science teacher at one of the local colleges. Miss Liu said that several of her close friends had attended some of the recent conferences in Peking. One, she said, went to the preparatory meeting of the People's Political Consultative Conference, another to a conference of scientists, and so forth. Without exception these friends returned to Nanking "changed people," their whole attitude having changed—"like Moral Rearmament," she said. At the conferences all attending had been asked to cooperate with the new regime and all had indicated a willingness to do so. Miss Liu said she had asked them whether they were not afraid of having to take orders from the USSR and all were vehement in their statements and belief that Chinese Communism is a Chinese movement under Chinese leadership, that there is no question of taking orders from Moscow. Miss Liu herself has evidently been impressed by the experiences of her friends, for people who know her well say that her attitude now seemed very different from that of a week ago when she still appeared to be opposed to the new regime. She said last night that she thought intellectuals should join the Communist Party so they could really know what is going on. I asked her what she thought the United Sates should do and she replied without hesitation that we should sever all connections with the Kuomintang and make it clear to all the world that we have done so.

We learned this morning that Ambassador Stuart now hopes to leave soon, and that he will leave suddenly when he does go. So I shall send this installment over to Major Van Ausdall to add to the collection of diary letters he is carrying with him. We have given up the idea of trying to leave China via Tientsin, even if we could get permission to go that way, now that there is serious talk of arranging with both Chinese governments for a ship to come into Shanghai to take out Americans who wish to leave. The railway trip to Shanghai has become dangerous because of Nationalist bombing and strafing, but the trip to Tientsin is arduous and expensive, and one cannot be certain of getting away from there even if we could get there.

I am continuing to work on the materials I have collected here. I have spoken on my research topic to a University of Nanking faculty group, and I am scheduled to speak on it again next Wednesday before the Nanking Research Club, recently revived by Frank A. Kierman,

Shirley Duncan, and some others. The USIS News Bulletin has been closed down by the Chinese authorities, but we are still able to listen to the BBC and Voice of America on the radio belonging to Miss Elsie Priest (Treasurer of the University of Nanking with whom we share the house we are living in). And there are lots of books about, which we read when it is too hot to work. We hope that we shall be able to leave sometime during the next month. There were early reports that the S.S. President Wilson might come into Shanghai next week, but we have heard nothing recently so I guess that was a false hope. Henry Lieberman of the *New York Times*, now in Shanghai, keeps me in touch with the latest news and rumors in that city.

There is today's fourth air raid alarm. Perhaps planes will really come this time. We hope that they will continue to miss the power plant and the water works) as well as defenseless people.

Notes

[1] For an excellent political and economic history of the Chinese civil war between 1945 and 1949 see Suzanne Pepper, *Civil War in China: The Political Struggle, 1945-1949* (Berkeley: University of California Press, 1978). Particularly important for the period covered by these letters are chapter 8 and 9. For the military aspects of this struggle see Lionel Max Chassin (translation from the French by Timothy Osato and Louis Gelas), *The Communist Conquest of China* (Cambridge: Harvard University Press, 1965), especially parts 4 and 5. There is much useful information in the so-called China White Paper: *United States Relations with China With Special Reference to the Period 1944-1949* (Washington: Department of State, 1949).

[2] I have changed Peiping to Peking throughout although the old name was not restored until September 27, 1949. I have also substituted surnames for given names, as Mrs. Biggerstaff (or Mrs. B) for Camilla.

[3] Derk Bodde, *Peking Diary: A Year of Revolution* (New York: Henry Schuman, Inc., 1950).

[4] A. Doak Barnett, *China on the Eve of Communist Takeover* (New York: Frederick A. Praeger, 1963), pp. 315-364.

[5] In *Two Chinas* (London: George Allen and Unwin, Ltd., 1955), pp. 32-63.

[6] Washington: Government Printing Office, vol. 8, 1978, Vol. 9, 1974.

[7] According to my pocket diary the price of rice doubled on April 4, for example, and the Nationalist currency several times lost a quarter or more of its purchasing power overnight. I obtained 17,500 "gold" yuan—the National Government's currency—for each U.S. dollar I exchanged on April 1, and 32,000 "gold" yuan for each U.S. dollar on April 21.

[8] I don't know how I happened not to describe this very important economic step at the time it was taken. In my July 15 letter I mentioned the temporary weakening of this savings system.

[9] For these protracted negotiations see *Foreign Relations of the United States, 1949*, 9. 1261 ff.

¹⁰ For a volume of letters written from Shanghai over a three and a half year period commencing April 29, 1949 by an American medical doctor who had practised there many years, see A. M. Dunlap, *Behind the Bamboo Curtain* (Washington: Public Affairs Press, 1956). This book and two others written by resident American newspaper reporters Lynn and Amos Landman, *Profile of Red China* (New York: Simon and Schuster, 1951), and Julian Schuman, *Assignment China* (New York: Whittier Books, Inc., 1956)—contain much interesting firsthand material on the liberation of Shanghai and events there during the next year or more. Dr. Dunlap tended to find developments disappointing after a short "honeymoon" period at the beginning whereas Mr. Schuman considered them quite promising.

¹¹ For detailed documentation of these episodes see *Foreign Relations of the United States, 1949*, 8. 723 ff.

¹² For her biography see Howard L. Boorman and Richard C. Howard, editors, *Biographical Dictionary of Republican China* (New York: Columbia University Press, 1970), 3. 460-462.

¹³ The present Foreign Minister of the People's Republic. For his biography see Donald M. Klein and Anne B. Clark, *Biographic Dictionary of Chinese Communism, 1921-1965* (Cambridge: Harvard University Press, 1971), 1. 393-395.

¹⁴ Eminent Chinese anthropologist. For his biography see Boorman and Howard, 2. 17-19.

¹⁵ For a report of rural conditions in this region filed by the U.S. consul-general in Shanghai on October 22, see *Foreign Relations of the United States, 1949*, 8. 557-559.

¹⁶ For his biography see Boorman and Howard, 3. 457-460.

¹⁷ William Olive, a U.S. consular officer in Shanghai, was arrested after violating a local traffic regulation and was somewhat roughly treated by the police. For more information see *Foreign Relations of the United States, 1949*, 8. 1199 ff.

The Nanking Press: April-September 1949

In Nanking's newspapers after "liberation" an American observer
finds clues to the new direction of Chinese thought and policy

By Knight Biggerstaff

THE CHINESE COMMUNISTS frankly regard the press as an
instrument of propaganda—as an important means of "educating" the
people. An examination of the Communist press can be enlightening
in its disclosure of the points the party is emphasizing at any given
moment and of the ideas it wishes to put into the minds of readers. The
present writer was in Nanking when the city was "liberated" by the
Communists on April 24, 1949 and remained there for the next five
months. Thus he had an opportunity to observe the first steps taken by
the Communists, and, by reading the local newspapers, to discover
what they wanted the populace to believe. What follows is a brief analysis of the Nanking press during the first five months of the new regime.

In the period immediately before the flight of the Central Government, some fifteen daily newspapers were published in Nanking. At
one time there had been a larger number, but several had died natural
deaths and others, most notably the outspoken *Hsin Min Pao* and
Nanking Jen Pao, had been suppressed by the authorities.

For a short time after the People's Liberation Army entered Nanking
a few of the pre-liberation newspapers, including the Catholic *I-shih
Pao*, the *Nanking Jih-pao*, and the *Chung-kuo Jih-pao*, continued to
appear, the employees of the newspapers in most cases having taken
over their operation from the former publishers. Even the official

Note: This article appeared in the *Far Eastern Survey*, March 8, 1950 (Volume XIX,
No. 5).

Kuomintang organ, the *Chung-yang Jih-pao*, appeared on the morning of April 24, startling its old readers with an enthusiastic welcome to the "liberators" and the attribution of most of its news to the Communist New China News Agency. During the following weeks more than a score of half-sized single-sheet newspapers were published, some for only two or three days, others for longer periods. The printing plant of the *Chung-yang Jih-pao* was taken over by the New China News Agency, which published a *Chieh-fang Hsin-wen* (Liberation News) for several days, but on April 30 changed the name to *Hsin Hua Jih-pao* (New China Daily). This has since continued to be the official organ of the new regime in Nanking.

May 17 was set as the final date for the registration of Chinese-language newspapers and on that day all papers ceased publication except the Hsin Hua Jih-pao and the *Chung-kuo Jih-pao* (China Daily). The latter, immediately prior to the liberation, had been regarded as the most independent newspaper published in Nanking. Later two other papers, suppressed by the former regime, were registered and began to appear: the *Hsin Min Pao* (New People's Paper), on June 3, after a lapse of almost ten months, and the *Nanking Jen Pao* (Nanking People's Paper) on July 7, after a lapse of more than five months. With the reopening of communications following the "liberation" of Shanghai on May 25, newspapers began to come in from that city once more. The Shanghai *Ta Kung Pao* (L'Impartial), in spite of a drastic change in its ideological orientation and modification of the traditional independence of its editorial page, remains the best newspaper in the region and the favorite of the more literate Nanking readers.

Purpose of Registration

On May 13, interim regulations governing the registration of Chinese-owned and Chinese-operated newspapers, magazines, and news agencies were issued by the Nanking Military Control Commission. These required, among other things, the filing of information regarding the present and past political views, records, and connections of the publishers and of all editors, correspondents, technical personnel, and stockholders. The declared purpose of registration was "to protect the people's freedom of speech and of the press, and to deprive anti-revolutionists of freedom of speech and of the press." Newspapers, magazines, and news agencies were forbidden by the regulations "(1) to violate the laws and regulations of the Control Commission or of the People's Government; (2) to carry on propaganda against the democratic activities of the people; (3) to divulge national or military secrets, or (4) to publish rumors or slander."

The *Hsin Hua Jih-pao* was the most widely read newspaper in Nanking. This was partly because it published all official proclamations and regulations (as well as a great deal of other material that literate people were expected to be familiar with), and partly because in addition to readers who bought or borrowed copies it reached a large audience through copies posted daily on walls at strategic locations throughout the city. It consisted of four full-sized pages—and occasionally of six or eight—in contrast to the four half-sized pages of the other local papers, and was well printed on good paper.

Most of the space in the *Hsin Hua Jih-pao* was given over to matters of national or local interest. Of primary importance and, in fact, the only parts of the newspaper read by many people were the official proclamations, instructions, and regulations already mentioned above. These ran all the way from instructions to report soldiers who tried to board buses or enter theaters without buying tickets, through local curfew, traffic, and other police regulations, to currency and foreign trade regulations, provisions for the establishment of national labor, youth, women's, and other such organizations, and the new Organic Law of the People's Democratic Republic of China.

Presumably no less important in the eyes of the authorities were the speeches and articles of prominent Communists and fellow-travelers and the biographies of military and political leaders. Most of the biographies appeared during the first weeks after liberation, but the speeches and articles, some of which had been delivered or written several years before, continued to be published in nearly every issue. Among the latter were policy statements by Mao Tze-tung, Liu Shao-chi, Chen Po-ta, and Liu Po-cheng—who was at that time mayor of Nanking. The speeches delivered at the opening of the meeting called to plan the Political Consultative Conference filled nearly half the space in the June 20 issue, and Mao's statement on the occasion of the 28th anniversary of the founding of the Chinese Communist Party took up the entire front page of the July 1 issue. Articles by little-known persons were given significance by the fact of their appearance in this official publication. The same may be said for the regularly unsigned editorials, which generally addressed themselves to some event of the moment such as a national youth or labor meeting, a conference on literature and the arts, or the Political Consultative Conference; or to some subject of current urgency such as the elimination of the black market in silver and foreign currencies or the necessity of converting Nanking from a city of parasitical government employees and their hangers-on into one of productive enterprise; or perhaps to some international topic.

Domestic news items, no less than speeches, feature articles, and editorials, were presented in such a way as to serve the cause of the New Democracy. News of the fighting was generally accurate, although the reports usually lagged several days behind the event. Supplementing the news were human interest stories describing the anti-social acts of Kuomintang soldiers and police before the liberation, the exemplary behavior of the People's Liberation Army, and the enthusiastic reception accorded the liberators everywhere. Although the news was generally optimistic, reports of failure, even of internal opposition, occasionally appeared. Unfavorable reports appear to have been published only when they could be made to serve a particular purpose. For example, although brief reports of local flood conditions had been published from time to time, it was not until July 13 that the extent of the disaster along the Yangtze and Yellow Rivers was disclosed, presumably at that particular time in order to explain food shortages and the resultant skyrocketing of prices. A favorite type of news story consisted of the reports of meetings of laborers, students, teachers, and other groups to welcome the liberators, to study the doctrines of the New Democracy, or to reorient the activities of members.

Reports of Achievement

No less common were reports of the achievements of this or that group: laborers who had saved machinery or vehicles from Kuomintang demolition; workers who had quickly repaired damaged railroads, mines, factories, and dykes; technicians who, after group study and discussion of Mao's New Democracy, had increased their production by working more efficiently, or for longer hours; students who enlisted in political cadres to serve in newly liberated areas, and so on. Other articles described various phases of the rehabilitation of Manchuria and of economic and educational developments in North China; and still others called attention to the improvement in popular living standards following the introduction of the People's currency or outlined new salary schedules for professors, officials, and other occupational groups. Membership lists of both local and national committees and other bodies and announcements of the names of students who had successfully passed examinations occupied considerable space in the daily press.

Almost every issue of the *Hsin Hua Jih-pao* included an article or two about the Soviet Union, the Communist satellite countries in eastern Europe, or Russian-dominated international organizations such as the World Federation of Trade Unions. Some of those were translated from the Russian, others were written directly in Chinese. Examples of the former were excerpts from the writings of Lenin, the May Day proclamation of the Central Executive Committee of the Russian Communist Party, an essay entitled "Our Pushkin," eulogies of the Bulgarian Communist Dimitrov, and articles on Russian labor organization, industrial development, education, cooperatives, etc., translated from Russian periodicals. Examples of the latter included articles on Gorki, Dimitrov, Russian music and drama, Russian leadership of international labor, and various aspects of the history of the Soviet Union and the "new democracies" of eastern Europe. Such writings were usually eulogistic in tone, never critical.

Ordinarily between a fifth and a fourth of the space in the *Hsin Hua Jih-pao* was given over to foreign and international news, with dispatches and articles covering the whole range of present-day Russian interest and showing undeviating adherence to the current Soviet line. Nearly all foreign news items carried the byline of the New China News Agency, but most of them also credited Tass or the Polish News Agency. American and other "imperialist" news sources were used only when, quoted out of context, they supported the Russian position, or when the quotation of partial truth served the same purpose.

The combination of Russian anti-Americanism and Chinese Communist bitterness over American aid to the Kuomintang resulted in studied distortion, and sometimes even in falsification, of news concerning the United States and its overseas activities. To illustrate: on the day the last American naval units were withdrawn from Tsingtao the *Hsin Hua Jih-pao* announced that large reinforcements of American naval craft had arrived in that port and that over a thousand marines had been put ashore; on another occasion it declared that Formosa had been purchased from Chiang Kai-shek by the United States for use as a military base; several times the American Secretary of State was charged with secretly negotiating a Pacific alliance similar to the North Atlantic Pact; and there was a steady campaign of charges that the United States was secretly rebuilding the Japanese army and encouraging the resumption of political and economic control of Japan by reactionary elements.

In reporting events within the United States the *Hsin Hua Jih-pao* faithfully followed the Moscow line—in fact nearly all such stories came through the Tass News Agency. Opposition to the Marshall Plan and to the North Atlantic Pact was played up to give the impression that a Wall Street-controlled government was forcing them upon an unwilling American people. Shortcomings in American democratic procedure and evidences of economic recession were spotlighted: favorite examples of the former were cases of racial discrimination, and typical of the latter were almost daily reports in June and July of drops in the stock market, increases in unemployment, and declines in commodity prices.

The "reactionary" character of the big American labor organizations was frequently alluded to, even while the strikes they called were described as desperate measures taken by the workers against their capitalist oppressors. One day a sympathetic story of a strike of Ford workers against the "speed-up" appeared on the same page with an account of the "voluntary" decision of the Nanking motor repair workers union to "repair more! repair better! repair faster!" Frequent accounts of the activities of the American Communist Party and of other "progressive elements" greatly magnified their importance and influence in the American scene.

Attack on White Paper

Release by the Department of State on August 5 of the White Paper on *United States Relations with China* touched off an almost hysterical anti-American outburst in the Nanking press. Not waiting to begin their campaign until they could secure a copy of this bulky document, the Chinese Communists for several weeks used the broadcast version of Secretary Acheson's Letter of Transmittal for ammunition. Day after day editorials, speeches, resolutions, and reports of round-table discussion groups and protest meetings were spread across the pages of the *Hsin Hua Jih-pao*, challenging American policy and the White Paper from every angle.

Particularly singled out for attack was Acheson's statement that "We continue to believe that . . . the profound civilization and the democratic individualism [which the Communists translated "democratic individualists"] of China will reassert themselves and she will throw off the foreign yoke. I consider that we should encourage all developments in China which . . . work toward this end." This was interpreted as an appeal to all Western-educated Chinese to work secretly against the new government and as a promise that such efforts would be aided by the American government. During a period of more than a month only one issue of the official newspaper failed to refer to the White Paper and sometimes extra pages had to be added to include all the attacks.

For a Chinese paper the *Hsin Hua Jih-pao* devoted an unusually large amount of space to European affairs, and persons familiar with Russian propaganda on the Marshall Plan, the North Atlantic "Aggression" Pact, the Conference of Foreign Ministers, and the German question found it faithfully reflected in this Nanking newspaper. Here also were the same vitriolic attacks on the anti-communist governments of Western Europe and on Tito, and the same explanations of the Greek and Italian situations as were published in Pravda and Izvestia. One invariably found the "peace-loving" USSR leading the propertyless peoples of Europe, and of the whole world for that matter, against the aggressive "secret plans" and actions of "Imperialist America" and its western European satellites.

The Russian propaganda line regarding Asia was no less faithfully followed. Nehru was declared to have sold out to American and British capitalism, thus betraying the Indian revolution; the invasion of the princely state of Hyderabad by the Indian army was portrayed as an act of aggression against the exploited masses; Hatta was also said to have sold out to American imperialism, thereby betraying not only Indonesia but all the peoples of southeast Asia; and South Korea, in contrast to "independent democratic" North Korea, was spoken of as a colony of the United States. Even with regard to the negotiation of a peace treaty with Japan, the Russian position that the small nations should be excluded and Russia and China have veto rights was maintained, on the ground that "China and Russia had made the principal contributions to Japan's defeat."

A substantial portion of each issue of the *Hsin Hua Jih-pao* was given over to stories, slogans, poems, songs, and cartoons praising Mao Tze-tung, the New Democracy, the People's Liberation Army, the laboring class, or some cause being pushed at the moment, or attacking Chiang Kai-shek and his reactionary associates, American imperialism, black market operators, or other enemies of the people. Historical sketches often depicted the struggles and achievements of early revolutionary heroes. A "letter box" welcomed criticism of all phases of life: speeding vehicles, official inefficiency, behavior of individuals and groups that was not in accord with the New Democracy; and answered questions ranging all the way from the time of train and bus departures, to problems of social ethics and political theory. Many letters suggesting improvements in the newspaper, in the city, and even in the administration of national affairs were published. Finally there was a daily chart of wholesale prices, and a half page or more of paid advertisements of theaters, shops, department stores, schools, etc., lost and found notices, and engagement, wedding, and divorce announcements. At least once a week a part or all of one page was devoted to the promotion of public health; and there was a weekly pictorial supplement, with pictures of public events and achievements of various kinds and sometimes propaganda cartoons.

Special issues of the *Hsin Hua Jih-pao* were published to commemorate such important days as International Labor Day (May 1) and the anniversaries of the founding of the Chinese Communist Party (July 1) the 1925 Shanghai Incident (May 30), the Japanese attack at the Marco Polo Bridge (July 7), and the signing in 1945 of the treaty between the Central Government of China and the USSR (August 14). In each case editorials, special feature articles, and songs, poems, and cartoons celebrating the event were included.

Although privately owned, the other three Nanking newspapers were little more than pint-sized versions of the *Hsin Hua Jih-pao*, for they included, as far as space limitations permitted, virtually all the types of material mentioned above. Some readers preferred them to the *Hsin Hua Jih-pao* primarily because their smaller size required them to be briefer in what they had to say and to leave out much of the duller propaganda carried by the official paper. But they derived all of their international and much of their Chinese news, and not a few of their feature articles and editorials, from the official New China News Agency. Moreover, they went out of their way to conform to the party line; in fact, some of the most malicious anti-American articles published in Nanking during the summer appeared in the small papers rather than in the *Hsin Hua Jih-pao*.

While the *Hsin Min Pao* maintained private wire connections with Shanghai and Peking and a small staff of its own reporters, thus supplying its readers with more of what we call "news" than the other papers, it was reported by the end of the summer to be in financial difficulties and to be applying for permission to close down. The *Chung-kuo Jih-pao* actually did cease publication for awhile, and may no longer be appearing. The political and economic decline of Nanking, combined with the new interpretation of what constitutes news, was rapidly making it financially impossible for any but government-supported newspapers to carry on.

Although the importance of Nanking appears to be slight in the eyes of the Chinese Communists, the intellectual fare offered to its people through the press after the "liberation" differed little from that reportedly supplied to the citizens of Shanghai, Hankow, Canton, and other central and south China cities. Not only was Communist news policy made in Peking but most of the copy originated there also. During the next few years as the government of the People's Democratic Republic of China struggles with the many problems it has fallen heir to, the material it releases for publication in the Chinese press will bear careful watching as an indication of the direction official policy may be expected to take.

CORNELL EAST ASIA SERIES

4 Fredrick Teiwes, *Provincial Leadership in China: The Cultural Revolution and Its Aftermath*

8 Cornelius C. Kubler, *Vocabulary and Notes to Ba Jin's* Jia: *An Aid for Reading the Novel*

16 Monica Bethe & Karen Brazell, *Nō as Performance: An Analysis of the Kuse Scene of* Yamamba

17 Royall Tyler, tr., *Pining Wind: A Cycle of Nō Plays*

18 Royall Tyler, tr., *Granny Mountains: A Second Cycle of Nō Plays*

23 Knight Biggerstaff, *Nanking Letters, 1949*

28 Diane E. Perushek, ed., *The Griffis Collection of Japanese Books: An Annotated Bibliography*

29 Monica Bethe & Karen Brazell, *Dance in the Nō Theater*
Vol. 1: Dance Analysis, Vol. 2: Plays and Scores, Vol. 3: Dance Patterns

32 A. Ronald Walton, *Tone, Segment, and Syllable in Chinese: A Poly-dimensional Approach to Surface Phonetic Structure*

36 Miwa Kai, tr., edited & annotated by Robert J. Smith & Kazuko Smith, *The Diary of a Japanese Innkeeper's Daughter*

37 J. Victor Koschmann, Ōiwa Keibō & Yamashita Shinji, eds., *International Perspectives on Yanagita Kunio and Japanese Folklore Studies*

38 James O'Brien, tr., *Murō Saisei: Three Works*

40 Kubo Sakae, *Land of Volcanic Ash: A Play in Two Parts,* revised edition, tr. David G. Goodman

41 Zhang Xinxin, *The Dreams of Our Generation and Selections from Beijing's People,* eds. & trs. Edward Gunn, Donna Jung & Patricia Farr

44 Susan Orpett Long, *Family Change and the Life Course in Japan*

46 Thomas P. Lyons & WANG Yan, *Planning and Finance in China's Economic Reforms*

48 Helen Craig McCullough, *Bungo Manual: Selected Reference Materials for Students of Classical Japanese*

49 Susan Blakeley Klein, *Ankoku Butō: The Premodern and Postmodern Influences on the Dance of Utter Darkness*

50 Karen Brazell, ed., *Twelve Plays of the Noh and Kyōgen Theaters*

51 David G. Goodman, ed., *Five Plays by Kishida Kunio*

52 Shirō Hara, *Ode to Stone,* tr. James Morita

53 Peter J. Katzenstein & Yutaka Tsujinaka, *Defending the Japanese State: Structures, Norms and the Political Responses to Terrorism and Violent Social Protest in the 1970s and 1980s*

54 Su Xiaokang & Wang Luxiang, *Deathsong of the River: A Reader's Guide to the Chinese TV Series* Heshang, trs. Richard Bodman & Pin P. Wan

55 Jingyuan Zhang, *Psychoanalysis in China: Literary Transformations, 1919-1949*

56 Jane Kate Leonard & John R. Watt, eds., *To Achieve Security and Wealth: The Qing Imperial State and the Economy, 1644-1911*

57 Andrew F. Jones, *Like a Knife: Ideology and Genre in Contemporary Chinese Popular Music*

58 Peter J. Katzenstein & Nobuo Okawara, *Japan's National Security: Structures, Norms and Policy Responses in a Changing World*

59 Carsten Holz, *The Role of Central Banking in China's Economic Reforms*

60 Chifumi Shimazaki, *Warrior Ghost Plays from the Japanese Noh Theater: Parallel Translations with Running Commentary*

61 Emily Groszos Ooms, *Women and Millenarian Protest in Meiji Japan: Deguchi Nao and Ōmotokyō*

62 Carolyn Anne Morley, *Transformation, Miracles, and Mischief: The Mountain Priest Plays of Kyōgen*

63 David R. McCann & Hyunjae Yee Sallee, tr., *Selected Poems of Kim Namjo*, afterword by Kim Yunsik

64 HUA Qingzhao, *From Yalta to Panmunjom: Truman's Diplomacy and the Four Powers, 1945-1953*

65 Margaret Benton Fukasawa, *Kitahara Hakushū: His Life and Poetry*

66 Kam Louie, ed., *Strange Tales from Strange Lands: Stories by Zheng Wanlong*, with introduction

67 Wang Wen-hsing, *Backed Against the Sea*, tr. Edward Gunn

68 Brother Anthony of Taizé & Young-Moo Kim, trs., *The Sound of My Waves: Selected Poems by Ko Un*

69 Brian Myers, *Han Sŏrya and North Korean Literature: The Failure of Socialist Realism in the DPRK*

70 Thomas P. Lyons & Victor Nee, eds., *The Economic Transformation of South China: Reform and Development in the Post-Mao Era*

71 David G. Goodman, tr., *After Apocalypse: Four Japanese Plays of Hiroshima and Nagasaki*, with introduction

72 Thomas P. Lyons, *Poverty and Growth in a South China County: Anxi, Fujian, 1949-1992*

73 Hwang Suk-Young, *The Shadow of Arms*, tr. Chun Kyung-Ja, foreword by Paik Nak-chung

74 Martyn Atkins, *Informal Empire in Crisis: British Diplomacy and the Chinese Customs Succession, 1927-1929*

75 Bishop D. McKendree, ed., *Barbed Wire and Rice: Poems and Songs from Japanese Prisoner-of-War Camps*

76 Chifumi Shimazaki, *Restless Spirits from Japanese Noh Plays of the Fourth Group: Parallel Translations with Running Commentary*

77 Brother Anthony of Taizé & Young-Moo Kim, trs., *Back to Heaven: Selected Poems of Ch'ŏn Sang Pyŏng*

78 Kevin O'Rourke, tr., *Singing Like a Cricket, Hooting Like an Owl: Selected Poems by Yi Kyu-bo*

79 Irit Averbuch, *The Gods Come Dancing: A Study of the Japanese Ritual Dance of Yamabushi Kagura*

80 Mark Peterson, *Korean Adoption and Inheritance: Case Studies in the Creation of a Classic Confucian Society*

81 Yenna Wu, tr., *The Lioness Roars: Shrew Stories from Late Imperial China*

82 Thomas Lyons, *The Economic Geography of Fujian: A Sourcebook*, Vol. 1

83 Pak Wan-so, *The Naked Tree*, tr. Yu Young-nan

84 C.T. Hsia, *The Classic Chinese Novel: A Critical Introduction*

85 Cho Chong-Rae, *Playing With Fire*, tr. Chun Kyung-Ja

86 Hayashi Fumiko, *I Saw a Pale Horse and Selections from Diary of a Vagabond*, tr. Janice Brown

87 Motoori Norinaga, *Kojiki-den, Book 1*, tr. Ann Wehmeyer

88 *Sending the Ship Out to the Stars: Poems of Park Je-chun*, tr. Chang Soo Ko

89 Thomas Lyons, *The Economic Geography of Fujian: A Sourcebook*, Vol. 2

90 Brother Anthony of Taizé, tr., *Midang: Early Lyrics of So Chong-Ju*

91 Chifumi Shimazaki, *Battle Noh: Parallel Translations with Running Commentary*

92 Janice Matsumura, *More Than a Momentary Nightmare: The Yokohama Incident and Wartime Japan*

93 Kim Jong-Gil, tr., *The Snow Falling on Chagall's Village: Selected Poems of Kim Ch'un-Su*

94 Wolhee Choe & Peter Fusco, trs., *Day-Shine: Poetry by Hyon-jong Chong*

95 Chifumi Shimazaki, *Troubled Souls from Japanese Noh Plays of the Fourth Group*

96 Hagiwara Sakutarō, *Principles of Poetry* (Shi no Genri), tr. Chester Wang

97 Mae Smethurst, *Dramatic Representations of Filial Piety: Five Noh in Translation*

98 Ross King, ed., *Description and Explanation in Korean Linguistics*

99 Richard J. Miller, *Japan's First Bureaucracy: A Study of Eighth-Century Government*, ed. Joan Piggott, revised edition

100 Yasushi Yamanouchi, J. Victor Koschmann and Ryūichi Narita, eds., *Total War and 'Modernization'*

101 Yi Ch'ŏng-jun, *The Prophet and Other Stories*, tr. Julie Pickering

102 S.A. Thornton, *Charisma and Community Formation in Medieval Japan: The Case of the Yugyō-ha (1300-1700)*

103 Sherman Cochran, ed., *Inventing Nanjing Road: Commercial Culture in Shanghai, 1900-1945*

104 Harold M. Tanner, *Strike Hard! Anti-Crime Campaigns and Chinese Criminal Justice, 1979-1985*

105 Brother Anthony of Taizé & Young-Moo Kim, trs., *Farmers' Dance: Poems by Shin Kyong-nim*

106 Susan Orpett Long, ed., *Lives in Motion: Composing Circles of Self and Community in Japan*

107 Peter J. Katzenstein, Natasha Hamilton-Hart, Kozo Kato, & Ming Yue, *Asian Regionalism*

FORTHCOMING

Pilwun Wang & Sarah Wang, *Early One Spring: A Learning Guide to Accompany the Film Video* February

John W. Hall & Toyoda Takeshi, eds., *Japan in the Muromachi Age*

Kenneth Alan Grossberg, *Japan's Renaissance: the Politics of the Muromachi Bakufu*

S. Yumiko Hulvey, *Ben no Naishi Nikki: A Poetic Record of Female Courtiers' Sacred Duties at the Kamakura-Period Court*

Don Kenny, *Kyōgen Women*

Yanghi Choe-Wall, *Vision of a Phoenix: The Poems of Hŏ Nansŏrhŏn*

Thomas Conlan, *In Little Need of Divine Intervention: Scrolls of the Mongol Invasions of Japan*

Brother Anthony of Taizé & Young-Moo Kim, trs., *Three Modern Korean Poets: Poems by Kim Su-yong, Shin Kyong-nim, Yi Si-yong*

To order, please contact the Cornell East Asia Series, East Asia Program, Cornell University, 140 Uris Hall, Ithaca, NY 14853-7601, USA; phone (607) 255-6222, fax (607) 255-1388, ceas@cornell.edu, http://www.einaudi.cornell.edu/eastasia/EastAsiaSeries.html.

3-00/.5 M pb